BETWEEN THE
LIGHTNING
AND THE
THUNDER

BETWEEN THE LIGHTNING AND THE THUNDER

Randy Storms

HARVEST HOUSE PUBLISHERS
Eugene, Oregon 97402

Some names have been changed in order to protect the privacy of the individuals involved.

BETWEEN THE LIGHTNING AND THE THUNDER

Copyright © 1989 by Randy Storms
Published by Harvest House Publishers
Eugene, Oregon 97402

Library of Congress Cataloging-in-Publication Data

Storms, Randy, 1956-
    Between the lightning and the thunder.

    1. Storms, Randy, 1956- . 2. Christian biography—United States. 3. Paraplegics—United States—Biography. 4. Paraplegia—Religious aspects—Christianity. I. Title.
BR1725.S827A3   1989   248.8'6'9024 [B]   88-83232
ISBN 0-89081-665-4

Printed in the United States of America.

To the Lord, the source and goal of my dream.

To Mom, Dad, and Melissa. Without your love, prayers, and support, I wouldn't be where I am today.

To the Southeast Young Life clubs of 1986-1989. Thanks for your acceptance and friendship, and for the memories.

Special thanks to Ed Stewart for skillfully and sensitively helping me tell my story.

CONTENTS

Introduction

//

I leave the house at about 11:15 A.M. and steer my old Ford van through the familiar streets of suburban Wichita, Kansas. The unpretentious brick homes and comfortable little shopping centers I pass are warm with hometown memories. Each intersection and landmark rustles the pages in the scrapbook of my memory which is jammed with thousands of faded snapshots of my childhood and youth.

I turn into the bus parking lane in front of Southeast High School. My routine for exiting the van is well-practiced, but it still takes a few minutes to perform. I unhook my wheelchair from behind the steering wheel and flip the switch which electronically opens the side door and unfolds the platform. Then I wheel onto the platform and flip another switch, lowering the platform to the sidewalk. I roll off the platform and guide my wheelchair to the rear of the van. A touch of the finger lifts the platform into the van and slides the door closed. I'd be lost without my van's electric motor and the battery of a big 18-wheeler which powers it.

I muscle my arm-powered wheelchair up the sidewalk to the school's main entrance. A tiny, frizzy-haired sophomore girl sees me coming and swings the glass door open. "Hi, Randy," she chirps cordially as she holds the door open for me.

"Hi, Jennifer," I return her cheery smile and scoot my chair through the opening. "How ya' doin' today?"

Jennifer walks alongside me toward the main hallway. "I just bombed on a history exam," she moans with a squint of pain. "I forgot to read one of the chapters. I'll be lucky to get a *D* on the test." Suddenly the frown is washed from Jennifer's face as she changes the subject. "But I have a great chance of making the sophomore cheerleading squad," she beams.

It isn't lunchtime yet, but the traffic in the halls is starting to build up. Jennifer raises her voice above the noisy chorus of hallway chatter, which is punctuated by locker doors slamming shut.

We reach the main intersection of the building. Jennifer waves a friendly good-bye and veers off to join her girlfriends. I park my wheelchair close to the center of the intersection, like a fisherman wading into a stream just far enough so the lure he casts can be seen by the greatest number of fish. In the next 20 to 30 minutes several hundred kids will walk past me on their way to and from lunch. From where I sit, I can see them and they can see me. Some stop to talk, like John, one of our Young Life club leaders who needs to discuss a couple of details about Wednesday night's meeting. Kristin also stops to give me a hug and tell me about her audition for a big part in the school play.

"Hey, Randy," a football player calls out above the din as he walks by. "Are you gonna be at the game Friday night?"

"I wouldn't miss seeing you play for anything, Travis," I call back as he disappears into the crowd.

Most of the kids at Southeast High School know me by sight, if not by name. In addition to spending most of my lunch hours here, I attend sports events, concerts, back-to-school nights—whatever happens to be going on which involves kids. Wherever I roll my chair on the campus, kids either stop to talk or smile and wave as they hurry by. There are still some who scurry past me with only a quick, suspicious glance. I read the same uncomfortable questions in each pair of furtive eyes: "How did a young guy like you end up in a wheelchair? Are you a 'retard' as well as a cripple? Why are you hanging around kids instead of people your age?" I hear those same silent questions wherever I travel to minister to kids: Young Life meetings, churches, school assemblies, camps, retreats. And wherever I tell my story, expressions of curiosity are changed to wonder and hope.

The minutes pass and so do dozens and dozens of noisy, lively Southeast students. I call their names, flash them friendly smiles, and laugh and joke with them. Some of the kids I see today, like Kristin and Travis, have found Christ through our Young Life club at Southeast. But many others, like Jennifer, still need to find Him. That's why I travel thousands of miles each year to churches, schools, and youth meetings. That's why I parked my wheelchair in the crowded halls of Southeast High School today. And that's why I'll be back tomorrow.

If somebody told me when I graduated from college that I would spend my life in ministry to teenagers, I would have called him crazy. If that person repeated his prophecy after the split-second accident which planted me in a wheelchair, I would have sent him away as a raving lunatic. I wouldn't have planned my life this way in a million years, nor would I wish the pain and struggles I have endured along the way on anyone in the world. Yet my life today is fulfilled so far beyond my wildest dreams that I can hardly believe it. It's incredible to me to think that God can use a guy in a wheelchair to reach kids for Him—but He's doing it!

That's why I want to tell my story to you. If God can use a guy in a wheelchair, whose youthful dreams were shattered forever by a tragic accident, then He can use anyone. It doesn't matter if you are disadvantaged or disabled in some way. Nobody has it all together. Everybody's life is touched by shattered dreams, lost opportunities, broken relationships, and tragic circumstances. But our God is the God of the new dream.

1

A Bright Horizon and Smooth Sailing

//

It was a dream game for me from the moment I led our team into the jam-packed gymnasium. The noisy crowd burst into deafening cheers as my 11 teammates and I trotted proudly onto the hardwood for pregame warm-ups. The raucous crowd, the blazing overhead lights, and the electric atmosphere of the tournament engulfed me. A shot of adrenaline surged through my system and I exulted in the moment. The crowd roared again as our opponents from Kinkaid High School charged onto the court and began their drills. Kinkaid's varsity basketball squad was undefeated and top-seeded in the tournament. They were big, fast, and talented. *A chance to beat the best!* I mused with relish as I launched practice shots from the perimeter. *This is what it's all about!*

From the opening tip-off I knew I was in for the game of my life. My heart pounded in my ears. The cheering was so thunderous that I could hardly hear the ball bounce off the floor as I dribbled down the court to set up our first play. The passing was crisp and true. I found an open spot in the defense, caught a snappy pass from our other guard, and sprung upward for a 15-footer. *Swish!*— two points. The Collegiate fans screamed their approval and I thought I could hear Dad and Mom yelling my name proudly.

Kinkaid streaked to the basket and scored, but we came right back down the court with another basket. For several minutes our teams swarmed up and down the court trading baskets. Then the Kinkaid defense started closing in on our forwards and center, leaving me open outside. The pass came out to me on the right side and I shot—*yes!* Then I was open on the left—*yes!* From the top of the key, then from the baseline, then a driving lay-up—*yes, yes, yes!* Basketball players pray for "the hot hand"—that fleeting and unpredictable ability to hit almost any shot. And that night I had it—everything was going in for me! I kept putting up the shots and they kept falling through the hoop.

My teammates were also hitting key shots and we played stingy defense. Kinkaid scrambled to keep up the pace, but it was our night and we slowly pulled away. When the final horn sounded, we leaped wildly into each other's arms as fans swarmed onto the court. It was the best game of my life and we had beaten the best team in the tournament. I scored 21 points that night, hitting 10 of 11 shots from the field, and we went on to win the tournament.

Like most athletes, the shelves of my memory are lined with exciting "highlight films" like these. But long before my exploits on the basketball court and the football field were memories, they were fanciful, larger-than-life childhood dreams. Some kids want to grow up to be police officers, firemen, ballet dancers, doctors, nurses, or cowboys; I always yearned to be a great athlete. During football season Joe Namath, the great quarterback for the New York Jets, was my idol. As an elementary-school kid my most treasured possessions were my shoulder pads, jersey, helmet, and football. To me every playground game was the Super Bowl, and I wanted every play to be a touchdown pass from Joe Namath to whichever of my buddies was playing Jets' hall-of-fame receiver Don Maynard.

During basketball season I was a rabid Boston Celtics' fan. I followed great Celtic players like John Havlicek, Sam Jones, and Bill Russell. I pretended that I was a member of the Celtics playing against Wilt Chamberlain and the Philadelphia 76ers for the NBA championship. I always made the last-second shot to win the game and beat Chamberlain, the legendary center from Kansas University in my home state.

I wanted to grow up to be a professional athlete. I was sure that scouts from the NFL and the NBA would hear of my boyhood sports triumphs in Wichita and show up at my front door begging me to sign a lucrative contract. I didn't care about a million-dollar salary; I just wanted the fame and glory of being the next Joe Namath or John Havlicek—and I knew I would be. My head was in the clouds, of course. I had no idea what it would take to fulfill my boyhood dreams. That's the way it is with our dreams sometimes, even when we grow into teenagers and adults. We fantasize and wish and hope, but we don't understand all the hard work which must accompany a dream to make it a reality.

I never played football with Joe Namath or basketball with John Havlicek, but I did play ball with a guy named Jack Chesky. Jack was a local hero—a talented athlete and my best friend.

Jack's family and my family have been close ever since I can remember. The Cheskys lived in Halstead, about 30 miles north of Wichita. Jack and I attended Wichita Collegiate School together, where my father was headmaster. During my freshman year in high school, Jack, a lofty junior, took me under his wing and we became like brothers. We were inseparable that year, spending almost every weekend together either at his house or mine.

Jack and I shared one big dream: sports. He was a scrappy competitor and a fiery leader who excelled in sports during his years at Collegiate. During my sophomore year Jack and I played varsity football and basketball together. Jack, a senior, was our number-one quarterback during football season, and I was first-string end and second-string quarterback. I was in awe of his ability, his competitiveness, and his character. Jack Chesky epitomized the successful athlete I was striving to become. But more than that, of all my peers Jack was the kind of person I wanted to be like. I respected his integrity and honesty, his diligence in sports and other endeavors, and his loyalty as a friend. Jack Chesky was the model big brother I never had.

Jack inspired me as an athlete more than anyone I've ever played with. During the first quarter of a big game against Norwich, I came back to the huddle after a play to find Jack crumpled on the turf, writhing in pain and holding his shoulder. After I helped move Jack to the sidelines, the coach said, "Storms, you're going in as quarterback for a couple of plays until Chesky feels better." I was terrified. Norwich was creaming us. I didn't want to play quarterback and get pounded by their burly linemen. Besides, in my mind being sent in to sub for Jack was like being asked to run plays for Joe Namath. Chesky was our leader, our spark plug, and our best athlete. I felt totally inadequate to fill his shoes, but I had no choice. So I ran the offense as quarterback for the rest of the first half. After every play I looked over to the sidelines to see if Jack was ready to come back in, but he was nowhere to be seen. The coach kept sending in plays for me to run.

During halftime I found Jack in the locker room. He was getting into his street clothes.

"Jack, what are you doing?" I demanded. "You may be a little banged up, but you can't quit."

"I'm not quitting," Jack explained, grimacing as he eased into his shirt. "The doc thinks I have a separated shoulder. I can't play at all. It looks like you're the number-one quarterback for the next few weeks."

"I can't do it, Jack; I'm not ready," I complained, trying to hide my feelings of panic.

"Don't worry, Randy, I'll help you," Jack encouraged. "You have the talent and you know the plays. I'll give you some pointers. You'll do a great job. Now get out there and take charge of that team, Sarge."

During the second half Jack stood on the sidelines with his arm in a sling, shouting encouragement to me with every play. I could feel my confidence rise every time I handled the ball. He kept calling me "Sarge," a nickname which stuck with me through high school and which the Chesky family still uses for me today. It was Jack's way of challenging me to be the boss, to rise to the occasion and fire up our team. Norwich rolled all over us that night, but with Jack cheering me on I scored a touchdown. It was the inauspicious beginning of a great football career for me at Collegiate. Jack's injury kept him out for the rest of the season, so I finished the schedule as starting quarterback. I went on to play starting quarterback in my junior and senior years.

After my sophomore football season, Jack and I stormed through the basketball season together as Collegiate's starting guards. Jack was the heart and soul of our team, a scrapper like my childhood idol John Havlicek. Jack was one of our smaller players, but he loved to mix it up inside with the big guys and fight for rebounds. Jack's ferocious inside ball-hawking and my outside shooting kept the teams in our league on their toes. We didn't win a championship that year, but we had a great competitive season. Thanks to Jack Chesky, my lifelong dreams of being a sports hero were coming true. I was a little sad as I watched Jack stride proudly across the platform on his graduation day. Our fantastic year as teammates was over. I exulted in our friendship, but I wished our dream season together could continue through my next two years at Collegiate.

As I left the campus on the last day of school, life ahead for me seemed to hold all the warmth and promise of the sun-drenched summer vacation which awaited me. I was standing on a mountaintop, and the horizon ahead was filled with even loftier peaks: triumphs in sports at Collegiate and beyond. I didn't see the small, dark cloud racing up behind me. The events of the first weeks of summer would send me tumbling down my mountain of exhilaration into a cold, gray valley of anguish.

Shortly after Jack's graduation I was on my way to a six-week tennis camp in Michigan with David Humphreys, another teammate of Jack's and mine that year. Even though he knew the camp would cut into our summer fun, Jack was excited that David and I could attend the camp. "You guys have a great camp," he urged with a smile, "and we'll make up for lost time when you get home from Michigan."

I plunged into tennis camp with all the fervor and fun which characterized my approach to sports. *I'm going to be the best tennis player this camp has ever seen—and have a blast doing it!* I plotted with anticipation. *The only way it could be any better is if Jack Chesky was here.* I couldn't help comparing my efforts on the court to what Jack would do if he had attended camp with me, but he had a job at home and was preparing for college in the fall.

On the fourth evening of camp I was in my room getting ready to turn in after a strenuous day of workouts. One of the counselors rapped on the door. "Randy, your dad is calling long-distance from Kansas." *This is strange,* I thought as I headed toward the office. *We just talked four days ago when he and Mom dropped me off for camp. Why would he call so soon?*

"Hi, Dad," I greeted him over the phone. "What's up?"

"Randy, I have some bad news," he began quietly, "and I don't know how to tell you." His quavering voice was tinged with grief and I immediately realized the seriousness of his message: Someone I knew had died. My mind raced through a dozen possibilities in a breathless, heart-stopping instant: *Mom or my sister, Melissa? One of my grandmothers? Somebody on the staff or faculty at the school?*

"What is it, Dad?" I asked in a cautious whisper, not really wanting to know.

"I'm at the Cheskys in Halstead," he replied. There was a long pause, and I sensed Dad's pain as he grasped for words. "Your friend Jack was in a terrible car crash last night. They tried to save him, Randy, but Jack died shortly after he arrived at the hospital."

The blow of Dad's words jarred me so that their meaning was momentarily blurred. My brain was instantly numb, like the heavy buzz I felt on the football field the second after my helmet cracked against the helmet or pads of another player. Dad's message left me stunned and emotionless. He carefully recited the details of the crash which had claimed the life of my best friend. I listened almost stoically, as if hearing a tragic news report involving someone I never knew.

Then Jack's dad, Vic, got on the phone. Still feeling emotionally paralyzed, I calmly expressed my condolences. I told him that I would be home for the funeral, but Vic objected. "I know you really want to be here with us, Randy," he began. His voice was touched with emotion, but he sounded confident. "But you know Jack wouldn't want you to interrupt tennis camp for him. He was proud of you, Randy, and he knew you were going to carry on his winning tradition at Collegiate. I think he would want you to stay at camp and give it all you've got."

As painful to me as his words were, Mr. Chesky was right. I could almost hear Jack saying, "Don't waste time crying over me, Sarge. You're going to be a tennis star at Collegiate and that camp is a great opportunity. Suck it up and go for it." So I agreed that I would stay in Michigan, assuring Vic that my thoughts and prayers were with him and his family.

I hung up the phone and sat down, dazed. David's parents, who were also good friends of the Cheskys, had called David at the same time that Dad called me. In a few minutes we found each other in the hall. Suddenly the shield of numb shock inside me crumbled and I fell into David's arms sobbing. We spent most of the night crying and talking about how we would miss Jack.

I felt terribly lost and alone for the next several days. I doggedly kept up with the activities of the camp program like Jack would expect me to do, but my heart wasn't in it. My imagination kept replaying a mental videotape of the accident as my dad had described it. I saw Jack's brother, Bill, driving him home to Halstead from Wichita late at night. Jack was asleep in the passenger's seat. My insides churned as I pictured the car racing toward the bridge outside Sedgwick. Suddenly the car careened out of control. *Bill! Jack! Watch out!* I screamed helplessly inside. The car skidded wildly. I could almost hear the screeching of the tires and the sickening crash of metal and glass on cement as the car slammed into the abutment. I cringed as I envisioned Jack's limp form trapped inside the twisted wreckage. Sirens screamed, red lights flashed, and Bill's desperate cry rose above the confusion: "My brother is hurt bad! Please help my brother!" I saw vivid images of paramedics hovering over my friend, frantically ministering to him as the ambulance squealed toward the hospital. Then I heard the doctor's somber, final pronouncement: "We did everything we could. He's gone." The words pounded into me repeatedly like a fist to my stomach.

Jack's death devastated me as much as if someone in my family had died. He was so full of life and had so much to live for. It was unfair. His accident didn't fit my rules for my life. God was tampering with my dream and I didn't like it. *Why did You take Jack away from me?* I demanded from God one afternoon as I blistered tennis ball after tennis ball over the net during serving practice. *How could You do this to me? My life has been unfolding according to plan. Everything was going my way. Jack was my inspiration. Then suddenly—wham!—he's gone and I'm left without a hero.*

I talked more to God in those weeks after Jack's death than I had in several years before it. Sure, I was a Christian. I grew up in a fine Christian family. We had Bible readings and prayers regularly. I had opened my life to Christ as a boy. But when I reached high school I didn't have much to talk to God about. My life was going great. I was already a star athlete at Collegiate. I had lots of friends and a great social life. And to top it all off, my dad was the headmaster of the school and mom was his right hand. I had no great, desperate needs, so I had quietly relegated God to the sidelines of my sports-oriented life. I showed up at church on Sunday mornings for Him, and I asked Him to watch over me on the basketball court or football field on Friday nights. Other than that, He was busy blessing the missionaries on the foreign fields, and I was busy making a name for myself at Collegiate. What did we have to talk about?

When Jack died I was hurt and angry, and I was pretty sure God was to blame for my feelings. Those weeks after Jack's death were filled with questions which were more vented in anger than asked. Staying in tennis camp that summer was probably the best thing I could have done. The rigorous schedule kept me occupied, and the tennis drills and matches gave me a positive outlet for the negative feelings which poked at my insides. Deep in my heart I knew that God must have had a good reason for allowing the accident, but I couldn't see it. By the end of the summer I had resigned myself to an uneasy truce in my relationship with God.

In response to Jack's death, I dedicated all my junior year sports activities to him. Also, at the beginning of that school year, our coach, Bill Carter, announced that two special awards—the Jack Chesky Sports Award and the Jack Chesky Leadership Award—would be presented at the end of the year. I desperately wanted to honor Jack's memory by being the first student at Collegiate to win those awards. So I played sports harder that year than ever before, and things really came together for our teams. We were 7-2 in football, and I passed for almost 1,000 yards with 12 touchdowns and a 55-percent completion rate. I starred on the basketball team, averaging about 25 points a game, and was named to the all-conference first team.

I was so sure that I would win the Chesky awards that I attended the awards ceremony with an acceptance speech ready in my mind. After dinner Coach Carter stepped to the podium to make the presentations, and I straightened my tie and cleared my throat to accept them. Coach Carter began, "Tonight it is my privilege to present the first annual Jack Chesky Sports Award and Leadership Award to Wichita Collegiate School's most deserving seniors . . ."

Seniors? I protested inside. *My Chesky awards are being presented to seniors?* Suddenly another ominous black shadow darkened my dreams. I had given my body and soul on the field, on the court, on the track, and in the classroom that year to win the Chesky awards. It was my final tribute to my best friend. I had earned those awards, but the staff decided that the Chesky awards would be senior awards. I was crushed. I wanted to win those awards more than anything in the world. It was a disappointment which took me weeks to overcome.

But in the true spirit of a competitor, I came back to Collegiate for my final year with a winner's attitude. My athletic dreams were tattered, but I was determined to etch my name in Collegiate's sports history. My senior year was almost as successful as my junior year, and I was privileged to be the first student at Collegiate to win both the Chesky Sports Award and the Chesky Leadership Award.

My football performance that year earned me some offers to play at the college level. Even though I liked football, I *loved* basketball. I still saw myself streaking down the polished parquet floor in Boston Gardens to sink the winning basket against Chamberlain and the 76ers. So I passed up some attractive football offers to accept a modest basketball scholarship from Austin College, a small school in Sherman, Texas.

I swaggered into Austin with big dreams and an even bigger ego. I was the hot-handed shooter who was going to put Austin's basketball program on the map. I threw myself into college athletics and social life with zest. But I bombed out badly on the basketball court—I couldn't even make the varsity squad at Austin. I was humiliated and dejected. I wasn't the "big man on campus" at Austin that I had planned to be. I was just another starry-eyed, cocky prep star who couldn't cut it in college-level hoops. My balloon of basketball stardom had burst in my face. At the end of the year I transferred to William Jewell College in Liberty, Missouri, where I played on the tennis team.

Even though my athletic horizons were clouded, I kept up my image of the fun-loving, party-going college man at Jewell. But the misplaced emphases and screwed-up priorities of my life to that point had begun to take their toll. I was skimming through a college education with no plan and no purpose for my life. Up until then I hadn't needed a plan. I had experienced success at practically everything I did without hardly trying. I had often been told that I got through high school on 70 percent talent and only 30 percent hard work. It was true. I didn't think too much about tomorrow unless I had a game to play or a party to crash. The only goals I had set for myself were in athletics—passing yardage in football, scoring average in basketball, this record in track, that skill in tennis. I was too busy enjoying life to worry about planning for my future.

But at Jewell the reality of life after college, and where God fit into it, began to crowd in on me. My perspective gradually changed, returning slowly to earth from my orbit of athletic idealism. I was no longer a sports star waiting to be discovered by the pros. I was just a college student trying to find his place in the world. I was finally beginning to grow up—something I hadn't done very much of—and settle down. I still partied into the wee hours on Saturday nights, but I was always in church on Sunday morning. After two years at Jewell I returned home to Wichita to complete a business degree at Friends University. Somewhere in the debris of my fall from the ivory tower of sports achievement, I found the Lord patiently waiting for me. Deep inside me the embers of my childhood faith began to glow again.

Standing on the steps of Friends University with a degree in my hands and nowhere to go, I had to face the real world. Athletics was still my dream, but my inter-collegiate playing days were over and there were no pro scouts asking for my autograph on a contract. All my memories of success were wrapped up in Collegiate School, so without considering many other options, I approached my dad about joining his staff as a teacher and a coach. I wasn't sure I wanted a career in teaching, but I warmed to the idea of assisting Coach Carter in the school's basketball program. Besides, Collegiate was a safe and secure environment—and I had an "in" with the boss. Dad and the board of directors enthusiastically welcomed me to the Collegiate faculty.

As I began teaching and coaching at Collegiate, things really began to settle into place for me. The athletic and social whirlwind of my high school and college days had diminished to a warm, breezy memory. I still enjoyed sports and spent lots of time with friends, but my life was finally revolving around a meaningful center: work-ing with kids. I taught seventh- and eighth-grade math and coached the junior high basketball team at Colle-giate. I discovered that I enjoyed being with kids in the social environment of junior high school. And they seemed to relate well to me, perhaps because I was closer to their age than other faculty members and still listened to their music. Besides, I was a something of a hero at Collegiate. Trophies adorned the showcases which my teams—with me as captain or star player—had won. Some of my school records still stood. The acclaim from my peers which had bolstered my self-esteem as an athlete was alive and well in my little junior high students.

By this time the deep inner pain I had suffered from Jack Chesky's tragic death had dwindled to a wistful memory. Reminders of Jack were everywhere: plaques, photographs, memorial awards. I walked the halls at Collegiate thinking about our great times together and wondering what he would be doing if he were still alive. I had changed so much since Jack died. How would he have changed? I still missed him like a big brother. I still yearned for his friendship. But I was confident that he would be proud of me for investing my energies in the school we both loved.

I had also settled down in my relationship with the Lord. The god of athletics I had so vigorously served in my teens was not dead, but at least its luster had been seriously tarnished through my experience. Yet the God I had accepted as a child was still with me, and I began to turn in His direction again. When I returned to Wichita from Jewell College I plugged into my home church, Eastminster Presbyterian. I became active in the Young Life ministry in Wichita by working in a high school club. God and I were not yet the best of friends, but at least we were on positive speaking terms.

During the spring of 1981, near the end of my second year of coaching at Collegiate, a great opportunity fanned the flames of my athletic fantasies. Coach Carter became the head basketball coach at Friends University in Wichita, and he asked me to take the job as his assistant coach. *Coaching at the college level*, I thought gleefully. *What a break!* I realized that, even though my dreams of being the next John Havlicek had faded, I still had a shot at being the next Red Auerbach, the legendary Boston Celtics' coach. I told Coach Carter that I was already committed for the summer, but I would seriously consider his offer for the fall.

As the school term ended that year I wasn't sure where I was headed, but I was excited about the possibilities. My life seemed to be taking off on its own again. All I had to do was ride the wave, and I liked where it was taking me. Jack Chesky's death, the great tragedy of my life, was far behind me. *I've already had my share of trouble. Nothing like that will touch me again*, I thought optimistically. I didn't realize how wrong I was.

My summer commitment was a job as director of a summer wilderness camp, called Woodfield Camp, on Lookout Mountain near Chattanooga, Tennessee. As I drove from Wichita to Chattanooga in June of 1981, I excitedly looked forward to the responsibilities of the new opportunity. Had I any hint of the serious life-changing challenge which awaited me there, I would have turned in my tracks and raced as far away from Woodfield Camp as I could get. But I drove on with innocent anticipation, with the God who knows and cares silently standing by within.

2

A Sudden, Terrifying Storm

///

Woodfield Camp is a beautiful spread of wooded wilderness surrounding a serene lake. The camp is a young adventurer's paradise complete with horseback riding, boating, swimming, fishing, and 500 mountainside acres to hike and explore. On Sunday, June 28, I and my staff of counselors welcomed a group of 45 energetic boys, ages 8 to 15, to our first week of summer camp at Woodfield.

My office and cabin were on one side of the lake and all the campers' cabins were on the other side. Each morning I would rise before anyone else to jog and work out. Then I would blow a few unmusical bugle blasts across the lake to wake up the campers and summon them down to the lake for their morning dip before breakfast.

The morning of Friday, July 3, is painted vividly in my memory. It was a typically cool, overcast morning, and a delicate shroud of fog blanketed the landscape around the lake. I rose early to run and exercise as usual. After my workout I sat down outside the camp office to drink in the beauty and stillness of the unspoiled morning. All too soon the silence would be shattered by a bugle blast and the raucous, joy-filled shouts of rowdy boys plunging into the lake. The delicate mist rolling in off the lake would give way to the piercing summer sun. This moment was quiet and special. I realize now that God was preparing me for the most terrifying day of my life with an interlude of silent wonder which I received almost breathlessly.

It was Independence Day weekend and there was a festive air about the day's activities. The morning mist yielded to a breathtaking, glorious summer day. The boys, the counselors, and I knocked ourselves out having fun. At about four o'clock I herded them up into the hills for the last activity of the afternoon, one of the highlights of the camp: the Woodfield obstacle course. Our obstacle course was a crude version of the superstars' obstacle course seen on TV. There was a maze of tires to prance through, a muddy water hazard to slog through, a huge oil bin to climb over, a ladder to scale and descend, trees to run around, etc. Every camper ran the course for time during the week trying to beat the "world's record." And for the boys, half the fun of running the course was getting dirty. Each boy finished his run covered with mud and sweat—and a smile of pleasure and conquest on his face.

I gave them all a pretty hard time that afternoon, playfully razzing them about how slowly they ran and how filthy they looked. So after they completed their runs, my youthful campers started leaning on me: "Come on, Randy, let's see you run the course. Try to break the world's record." I told them that I would love to run the course, but I couldn't do it because I had "major administrative duties" I had to take care of. The truth of the matter was that I didn't want to get dirty! But these guys wouldn't take no for an answer. They blocked my path back to the office and said they weren't going to let me go until I ran the course. It was all in good-natured fun, however, and I could have weaseled out of running the course if I really wanted to. But I had never backed down from an athletic challenge in my life, and I wasn't going to do so now. It was another opportunity to live my dream and prove myself as the consummate jock. "Okay," I gave in, "I'll give it my best shot." I handed the stopwatch to one of the guys and stepped to the starting line, to the robust cheers of the mud-streaked onlookers.

That moment, as I stood ready to start my run, is frozen crystal clear in my mind. I scanned my surroundings and absorbed the beautiful scene, much like I had done that morning beside the misty lake. The sky was laser-blue and the late-afternoon sun blazed through the trees, splashing the mountainside with brilliant light. I felt so alive, so in control of myself and my life. I was 24 years old and in top physical condition. I had a wonderful family and many great friends and adoring students. I had a promising future in coaching which could help me fulfill my lifelong dream for a career in the world of sports. And to top it all off, God was in my life, although I was still rather self-assured, so I hadn't found much practical use for Him yet.

I took a deep breath and signaled to the timekeeper that I was ready to go. Within seconds my athletic dreams would be shattered and my need for my family, my friends, and God would be greater than I ever imagined. My muscular legs braced to launch me on the last race I would ever run.

Someone yelled "Go!" and I bolted down the path toward the first obstacle: a double row of tires on the ground. I danced quickly through the tires as I had done countless times on the football practice field. My adrenaline was pumping as I anticipated the acclaim of the campers for breaking the world's record for the course.

The second obstacle was a mudhole about eight feet long and four feet deep with a bar stretched across the middle at the surface. The object was to jump into the muddy water and crawl under the bar as fast as possible—and you couldn't do it without getting covered with slime and mud.

These guys can't wait to see me wallowing in that muddy gunk, I thought as I cleared the last tires, hearing the hoots and howls of anticipation from the watching campers. *Well, I'll show them a splash they'll never forget.* I determined that the quickest way to get through the mudhole was to hit it headfirst on a flying dive and swoop under the bar in the murky water. Looking back, I should have used better sense, but I didn't. It was one of those foolhardy, instantaneous decisions we make without considering the possible dangerous consequences. Sometimes we make thoughtless decisions and get away with them, but my split-second choice to dive instead of jump would drastically and irreversibly change my life.

About ten feet of muddy turf separated the tires from the mudhole, so I sprinted—slipping and sliding—away from the tires and dove recklessly into the mudhole. But I dove too deeply and my chin slammed hard against the bottom. I felt a snap in my neck and blacked out for a couple of seconds. When I came to, I was facedown under two feet of muddy water and completely numb. I frantically tried to raise my head for air, but I couldn't. I struggled to lift my arms and kick my legs, but nothing would move. Muddy water filled my mouth and nose, choking me. To my horror I realized that the campers and counselors watching me probably thought this was just another one of my stunts for getting attention. *They don't even know I'm in trouble!* my mind screamed in panic. *I'm going to drown if I don't cry for help!*

Again I tried to thrust my head above the water and failed. Finally, in a desperate third attempt, I yanked my head out of the muddy water. "Help me!" I gasped frantically before slipping underwater again. Suddenly the water churned around me as a couple of guys plunged in and a flurry of hands and arms clumsily wrestled me out. I was panting and coughing, and my heart pounded wildly from the trauma of nearly drowning. My head was fuzzy from the blow on the chin and my body was smeared with mud from head to toe. Below the neck I had no feeling and no pain. "I can't move anything; something's really wrong," I sputtered breathlessly. "Get some help up here!"

Somebody sprinted off to call an ambulance. I was lying motionless on my back beside the mudhole trying desperately to move my limbs. It was the classic night-mare of facing great danger and being unable to run away—except I wasn't asleep; my nightmare was real. I repeatedly willed my arms and legs to move, but they would not obey. My mind raced in a hundred directions wondering what had happened to me and how serious my injury was. I felt terribly helpless, afraid, and out of control, and I fought back waves of hysteria.

The gang of wide-eyed campers and counselors hud-dled around me wanting to help, but fearing to move me. Their faces mirrored my trauma. "Everything is going to be okay, Randy," they promised hopefully as we always do when we don't know what to say. I wanted to believe them. *The numbness is only temporary*, my blurred thoughts told me as I groped for a foothold of hope. *I know it's happened before in sports: a traumatic injury which results in temporary*—my mind blocked out the word "paralysis"—*loss of feeling. Soon I'll feel the pins and needles all over me, and I'll be on my feet before the paramedics arrive.*

But it didn't happen. "Do you feel anything now?" a young paramedic asked as he knelt in the mud near my feet.

"I don't feel anything, " I answered as calmly as I could. "What are you doing?"

"I'm poking your feet with the end of my pen," the attendant replied. "Can you feel my pen poking your foot?"

I want to feel something, I must feel something, I begged inside. I strained for some hopeful sensation. "Not yet," I sighed finally.

The late-afternoon shadows stretched across the moun-tainside as the paramedics carefully strapped my limp, mud-caked frame to a body board and loaded me into the ambulance. *Everything is very, very wrong*, I protested inside. *I have a camp to run. I have boys to take care of. I can't, I can't* . . . Wisps of silent darkness began to drift through my brain. The sounds around me—the farewells of the campers, the ambulance doors slamming shut, the engine revving to life—faded into the distance. My eyelids drooped heavily. I was vaguely aware that the paramedic attending me was trying his best to keep me awake. I struggled to comply, but somewhere between Woodfield Camp and Erlanger Hospital in Chattanooga, giant, cold waves of shock washed over me and swept me into unconscious blackness.

I awakened groggy and disoriented at about 11:00 that night. My body was immobilized in traction in a hospital bed. There seemed to be a thick layer of cotton between my consciousness and reality. The room was sterile and colorless, dimly washed with fluorescent light. The muted *beeps* and *clicks* of life-monitoring equipment surrounded me. My grainy eyes gradually focused on the sober faces of my parents, Randall and Betty Storms, and my sister, Melissa, bending over me.

I was unaware of the almost unbearable nightmare of anguish my family had suffered during my six hours of unconsciousness. By the time I arrived at the neuro-intensive-care unit, my vital signs had dipped dangerously low. The first doctors who worked on me offered little hope for my survival. One of them reached my parents by phone at their summer home in North Carolina. "Your son has suffered a tragic accident and broken his neck," he told them. "He is still alive, but we don't expect him to live through the night. And if he does make it through the night, he probably won't survive the weekend. If you want to see him alive, you'd better get here as soon as possible."

Deeply shocked and distressed, my parents immediately chartered a plane for Chattanooga, prayerfully hoping against slim hope that they would arrive in time to see me before I died. My sister, Melissa, was also notified, and she rushed to Chattanooga from Wichita. The doctors had painted my scenario in the darkest colors. I had no idea how much joy I brought to my family that night when my eyes slowly opened.

I was far from being fully conscious or alert the next morning when the serious-faced doctor walked into my room. Dad, Mom, and Melissa gathered around my bed as he recited the bad news: "Randy, you've suffered the most tragic accident a person can possibly suffer and still be alive. You've broken your neck at the sixth vertebra. You are paralyzed from the mid-chest down and you'll never walk again." I heard what he said, but the hangover of shock and trauma from the injury still clouded my brain. I didn't fully understand the severity of my condition.

But my mom understood the situation, and she also understood the power of God. "Doctor, the Lord hasn't said my son won't walk again," she said kindly but firmly, "so we will wait for His direction on the issue." The rest of the family nodded in agreement. My family's rock-solid faith, as typified by my mother's statement, was to serve as a foundation for my long, arduous recovery over the next several months.

I remained in critical condition through the weekend, with the added complication of pneumonia setting in on Sunday. I was so sick and "out of it" mentally that I did little more than exist. I faintly remember my family coming in to see me a couple of times a day, which was all they were permitted. They spent the intervening hours huddled tearfully in the waiting room, vigilantly supporting me in prayer. Rev. Ben Haden, pastor of the First Presbyterian Church in Chattanooga, heard about my accident from some of his parishioners and rushed to the hospital. He didn't know me or my family, but he became a tower of strength and comfort to us in those first few days. Mom remembers Rev. Haden exhorting them to prayer by saying, "Let's storm the gates of heaven for Randy Storms." He wept with my grief-stricken parents as if he had known our family all his life. I thank God for Rev. Haden's responsiveness, and I cherish his friendship today.

During those first several days in intensive care, I didn't have the energy or concentration to think about the long-term effects of my accident. I was too busy battling pneumonia and the moment-to-moment discomfort of total immobility and traction. One of my most painful memories from that first week was of the instrument used to immobilize my head and keep pressure off my broken neck. The device looked like a pair of stainless steel tongs, the kind used to move huge blocks of ice. The two sharp, pointed tips were imbedded on either side of my skull just above the temples to keep my head from moving. I must have looked like something from outer space with those stainless-steel appendages curving out from my brain. Every so often the sharp tips would work free and the doctors would have to press them back into place to keep my head stationary. It was very painful.

By the end of my first week in ICU, I was starting to feel halfway human again. I was still completely immobilized and my brain was still a little fuzzy, but I had this insatiable craving. "I'm hungry for pizza," I told my parents and sister when they came into my room.

"You want what?" they asked in disbelief. I told them about a pizza place in Chattanooga called Charley's which I had frequented before my injury. I was barely on a solid-food diet, but I just had to have some of Charley's pizza. So Melissa went down to Charley's and ordered me a pizza, and that night we had a family pizza party in the intensive care unit. Eating pizza while lying flat on your back is a real challenge—especially when somebody else is feeding it to you. But it tasted so good, and the party atmosphere really lifted our spirits. We knew we had some trying times ahead, but we were relieved that the life-threatening crisis of those first days in the hospital was over.

Near the end of my first week at Erlanger the doctors announced that surgery was necessary to fuse my neck at the point of the break. I was beginning to grasp the severity of my condition, and every shred of truth about the prognosis terrified me anew. Everyone was talking so positively and praying so fervently that I didn't dare express the worrisome fears which were slowly overcoming me. But neck surgery seemed like another frightful blot on the formless, dark future which seemed to hover over me in my helpless state.

On the night before surgery, a group of my dearest loved ones gathered around my bed to pray with me. There was Dad; Mom; Melissa; Dr. Frank Kik, my pastor from Eastminster Presbyterian Church in Wichita; and Bob and Lil Love, long-time family friends from Wichita. The informal prayer meeting was a sweet and special time which was very meaningful to me. I was humbled by the fact that these dear people would come all the way to Chattanooga to minister to me.

"I have something special for you, Randy," Frank announced after prayers. He lifted a huge scrapbook over my bed so I could see it. "Last Monday night we held a special prayer service for you in the chapel at Collegiate. About 500 people showed up just to pray for your recovery: your friends, your students and fellow faculty members, church members, and people from the community. They filled this scrapbook with notes of love, prayers, and best wishes. They want you to know that they're with you all the way."

Frank's words really blew me away. "Five hundred people came out to pray for me?" I asked disbelievingly, tears filling my eyes.

"Not only that, Randy," Frank continued, "but the news about your accident has spread to churches all around the country. Just as we prayed here tonight, there is a literal army of Christians across America holding you up in prayer. The Lord has you covered, Randy—believe me."

Frank flipped through the pages of the scrapbook so I could read some of the entries, but tears of wonder blurred my vision. Some had written prayers, others had simply scrawled words of encouragement or signed their names. Some of the names in the book I didn't even know. The scrapbook remains a priceless treasure to me to this day.

Later that night after everyone had left, I was lying in bed with my mind churning about the surgery which awaited me the next morning. Somewhere in the back of my brain a frail but persistent optimism tried to assure me that surgery was going to make me well. I had felt a similar kind of optimism as an athlete—on a much smaller scale, of course. It was the feeling of knowing you can still win a basketball game even though your team is ten points behind with only a minute left to play. I knew that miraculous, last-minute, against-all-odds victories were possible. So I hoped that the surgery would miraculously cause waves of feeling to surge back into my limbs, and that I would walk out of the hospital in a couple of weeks on my own two feet. The problem was that nobody else, including the surgeons, had offered me any grounds for that hope. The surgery was for the purpose of stabilizing my neck—period. A persistent knot twisted painfully in my gut. I was afraid to admit it to myself or anyone else, but I was afraid that I might never be well again.

I was lying in the semidarkness, refereeing the wrestling match between my hopes and my fears, when my night nurse, a man in his late 20s named Bobby, came into my room. Bobby is one of the most gentle, loving, and kind Christians I have ever been around. I knew he wasn't just making small talk when he looked me straight in the eyes and asked, "How are you doing?"

Up until that moment I had held up a pretty strong front, assuring myself and everyone else that I was going to be fine. After all, how could I contradict what everybody else was saying? "Don't worry, Randy, we're praying for you"; "Think positively; you'll be back on your feet in no time"; "The Lord is with you, Randy, and He will heal you." Intellectually I knew that people were praying for me. Intellectually I knew that I was in the greatest hands possible. Intellectually I knew that God could miraculously reverse my injury and make me completely well. But Bobby wasn't asking how I was doing intellectually; he was asking how I was doing emotionally. The suppressed fears I had held at bay for six days finally welled up into my throat and I began to cry. "I'm scared to death, Bobby," I sobbed. "I'm afraid of what's going to happen to me. I'm afraid I may never walk again."

Bobby held my hand tenderly and listened compassionately as I poured out my fears. Then he wiped the tears from my cheeks. Bobby didn't try to pump me up with a lot of platitudes or false hopes. He just prayed that God would meet me where I was: "Lord, Randy is really hurting right now. He's worried and afraid about what's going to happen to him. But You know where he is, Lord, and You love him so much. Give Randy Your peace, Your comfort, and Your strength for the operation tomorrow and the days beyond. Help him to know that he is always in the palm of Your hand."

Bobby's prayer was one of the most comforting, sustaining prayers anybody has ever prayed for me. He talked to God like He was his best friend, like He was standing beside the bed right with us. I felt a sense of calm wash over me and I slept in His peace that night.

During my recovery from surgery I had a lot of time to think. As my mind plodded through the factual data of what had happened to me and the projections for my future, my feelings continually rode the elevator from the basement of depression to the penthouse of confidence and back down again.

I finally came to grips with the fact that my physical injury was serious. There was nothing I could do to change it. My dreams and hopes for a life centered on athletics had been shattered in an instant at the bottom of a mudhole. I replayed the mental tape of my accident repeatedly, just as I had mentally relived Jack Chesky's fatal crash several years earlier. But the vivid scene in my memory of me racing toward the mudhole was not imagined from a report I heard. I was there. It happened to me. It was my decision to dive into the mudhole and it was my neck which was broken. I chastised myself mercilessly for making such a foolish choice, but for all the anger and regret I felt, I knew I could not reverse what had happened.

Furthermore, I acknowledged that I was now, and would be for my lifetime, a different person. For all intents and purposes I was a 24-year-old baby. Somebody had to clothe me, bathe me, and feed me. If I had an itch, somebody else had to scratch it. There was virtually nothing I could do for myself. It was very humbling, and at times very frightening, to realize that I was no longer in control of my life. Even though in my head I knew that the Lord was going to carry me through the ordeal, in my heart I was afraid of the many unknowns which awaited me on the untraveled road ahead.

I also thought about the frail and fleeting nature of the human body. We live in a society of people today who go all out; the more dangerous the life-style the better. We tend to forget that the human body is not indestructible. Any number of seemingly harmless activities—driving a car, playing a sport, using a power tool, etc.—can result in a tragic, irreversibly debilitating injury or death. Jack Chesky's accident had burned the reality of that fact into me years earlier. You can make one tiny mistake and be maimed for life. I thought about all the times that I could have been hurt playing football or basketball. Somehow I made it through my playing days in one piece, but it only took a little dive into a mudhole to change me from an active sports participant to a spectator.

Psalm 103 describes man as a fragile flower which is blown away as quickly as it sprouts and blooms. That's a very humbling description. Our egos are so incredibly huge, and yet we have nothing to be egotistical about—not one thing! Everything we have is a gift from God, including our health, our strength, and life itself. If we could just realize that we're here on borrowed time and borrowed abilities. Physical life can be limited or terminated in an instant. What's really important in our lives is not the shell, but what's inside the shell: the condition of our hearts. My accident caused me to realize that I had sold myself short for 24 years. I had based my life on physical skills and athletic goals and dreams. No matter how healthy, strong, or physically talented you may be today, be sure that your body is already on a collision course with ultimate destruction. Only what you do to build up the inside is going to last.

I had plenty of time to think about the big question: Why? It's the question we all ask when we are the victims of a tragedy, whether it's the death of a friend, a breakup in the family, or an accident like I had. Everybody goes through tragedies, and some are greater than others. We're all tempted to hold God responsible and demand that He explain to our satisfaction why it happened to us.

When the severity of my injury began to dawn on me, I wanted to shake my fist at God and say, "Hey! Why did You let this happen to me? You allowed the whole direction of my life to change in a split-second. You allowed my athletic dreams to be completely shattered. You took away the most precious thing in the world to me. Why? Why? Why?"

But in my head I knew that if I sat around grumping at God, waiting for Him to answer all my why questions, I'd be sitting around for a long time. My accident, and the paralysis it produced, was a test of my character which God had allowed but hadn't fully explained. And like any good teacher, God wasn't passing out the answer sheet while the test was still in progress. If He gave me the answers ahead of time, I wouldn't learn anything from the test. The answers to these tests only come little by little as we journey onward seeking the Lord, searching out His Word, and growing in our relationship with Him. We will only learn the answers while we're in the process of taking the test, even though that process isn't always fun. Some of these tests—like mine, for instance—may carry on for years, or even for a lifetime.

And so, very early in my recovery, I realized that a battle line was being drawn inside me. On one side, my intellect was in charge and its army was well-established and formidable. I had been taught from childhood that God is sovereign: all-knowing, all-powerful, and ever-present. Nothing happens apart from His knowledge or outside His jurisdiction. God is also in control of what He rules. Nothing happens that He doesn't cause or permit. Furthermore, intellect reminded me that the sovereign God is also a loving God. What He causes and permits in our lives reflects His love for us. God's perfect love knows what is best for us, and God's sovereignty causes or permits only those things in our lives which fulfill His loving purpose for us.

As I lay immobile on my bed in Erlanger Hospital, my intellect—buoyed by the prayers and encouragement of my loved ones—came up with all the right answers: A loving, sovereign God has allowed my accident for reasons beyond my understanding. There's absolutely nothing I can do to reverse the situation. I have no grounds to ask, "Why?" rather I must ask, "Where do we go from here?"

But there was another powerful army on the other side of the line ready to battle my intellect for supremacy in response to my injury. My emotions were not well-organized and predictable like my intellect. Rather, my feelings were like an army of guerrillas sneaking across the lines to cripple the enemy with surprise attacks. My feelings riddled my intellect with sniper fire, mostly in the form of questions: *What did I do to deserve this? Couldn't God teach me what He wanted to teach me without paralyzing me? Did He have to take away what I loved most: my physical ability and my athletics?* As I thought about spending the rest of my life in a wheelchair, my head said, "Trust God and He will bring something good out of this." But my hostile emotions shot back, "What good can possibly come out of a broken-down athlete confined to a wheelchair?" Similarly, every positive, faith-induced element of God's involvement and control in my injury became the target of my fear and self-pity. Just as the scraggly, disorganized, pot-shooting colonists decimated the neat rows of British troops in the American Revolution, my subversive emotions had my intellect on the run.

I heard a story recently which illustrates the unexpected conflict which ignited in me during those first days after my injury. A schoolteacher lost his wife to cancer, and he was so grieved by his wife's death that he couldn't come back to school. He was a Christian and a popular teacher who was loved by everyone at the school, but his pain was so great that he just couldn't teach. His feelings threatened to undermine the foundation of what he knew to be true about God and His will.

On the last day of school all the students were gathered in the auditorium for graduation. Suddenly the back doors swung open and the grieving teacher walked in. He made his way down the aisle to the front of the auditorium and faced the graduating class. The students knew about his tragedy, and the auditorium was hushed as they awaited his words. Tears flooded his eyes as he uttered three simple sentences which said it all: "I hit the bottom. But the bottom was solid. The bottom was Jesus Christ."

Intellectually, I had a similar testimony. On July 3, 1981, I hit the bottom of a mudhole and the bottom of my life. But the bottom was solid. The bottom was Jesus

Christ. Unfortunately I had some angry, hurt feelings which were not about to surrender so easily. As I prepared to leave Erlanger Hospital for extensive rehabilitation, the battle between what I knew and what I felt raged on. I wondered what life could hold for a 24-year-old, broken-down, former athlete.

3

Lingering Clouds and Glimmers of Sunlight

//

About two weeks after neck surgery at Erlanger Hospital, something happened which brought me face-to-face with the stark reality of my condition and the grueling task of rehabilitation ahead of me. The movie playing on TV one night was an all-time favorite of mine, *The Other Side of the Mountain*. It's the true story of Jill Kinmont, the American skier who crashed during the Olympic trials in 1955, breaking her neck at about the same place mine is broken. I had seen the movie before my accident and admired Jill's courage and determination in overcoming her serious handicap.

This time I watched the movie from an entirely different perspective. Instead of seeing Jill Kinmont on the screen, I saw myself, prompting an eruption of deep, sorrowful tears. As she stood at the gate awaiting the start of her fateful downhill run, I saw myself poised on the starting line of the obstacle course. *Don't do it; don't go*, I begged the images on the screen and in my memory, writhing in futility over the tragedies I could not prevent. The footage of her violent, high-speed crash on the ski slope revived the haunting memories of my foolhardy dive into the mudhole. Watching her agonize through the realization of her paralysis painfully uncovered repressed fears that I would never walk again. Scenes detailing her slow and strenuous rehabilitation taunted me about the steep road to recovery lying ahead of me. I've never cried so hard in my life as when I watched that movie in Erlanger Hospital. I knew that my tedious journey had only just begun.

Since my accident I have learned that, up until 25-30 years ago, most victims of serious spinal cord injuries like Jill Kinmont's and mine died at the scene of the accident. Many of those who did make it to hospital emergency rooms expired within the first 24 hours. Thankfully, advances in medical science have drastically altered those statistics. More and more accident victims are surviving to face life as paraplegics and quadriplegics. But the good news of the increased survival rate was accompanied by a sobering question in the medical community: What shall we do with all these people who can't walk, feed themselves, or groom themselves? The answers to questions like these have given rise to a relatively new branch of specialized medicine dealing with rehabilitative therapy for the victims of spinal cord injuries. One of the premier institutions in the country equipping paras and quads to deal with their limitations is the Rocky Mountain Spinal Cord Center at Craig Hospital in Englewood, Colorado.

After a month of recovery in Erlanger Hospital in Chattanooga, I was transferred to Craig Hospital in the Denver suburbs. Russ Meyer, a family friend and chairman of the board of the Cessna Corporation headquartered in Wichita, graciously provided my transportation to Denver in his private jet. I had beaten the early odds against me and survived my accident. Now it was time to begin the task of learning to live as a quadriplegic. I would spend more than three months at Craig Hospital in extensive physical and occupational therapy.

One of the main reasons I survived my broken neck was my physical condition at the time of the accident. I was in great shape. In addition to the physical activity connected with coaching and directing the camp, I had been jogging, working out, and teaching an aerobics class. The doctors admitted that my disciplined attention to rigorous physical conditioning had saved my life during the first critical weekend.

But by the time I arrived at Craig Hospital I was in terrible shape. My accident and a month of virtual dormancy in a hospital bed had transformed me from a specimen of physical strength into a physical wreck. My weight had plummeted from 175 to 125 pounds. My arm muscles, over which I still retained some control, were so stiff and tight from atrophy that I couldn't even lift a Lifesaver to my mouth.

I was in even worse shape emotionally. Deep inside my pathetic-looking frame, I was as scared as a kid on his first day in kindergarten. I was entering a world I knew practically nothing about, a world of permanently broken human beings trying to regain some semblance of normalcy for their lives. I saw people in wheelchairs everywhere—paraplegics and quadriplegics. Some of them wore large stainless-steel hoops around their heads to stabilize their necks. Each "halo" was attached to the head by four rods bored into the skull. The sight of these freakish contraptions turned me cold with fear.

Craig Hospital is also a treatment center for victims of brain damage, and many of these patients rolled through the halls with blank or distant expressions. Their brain injuries had robbed them of various mental functions as well as motor functions. The shock of being around these people made me realize that I had lived 24 years sheltered in a virtual utopia of physical and mental strength. Suddenly I was submerged in a tiny subculture of broken people I never knew existed—and I was one of them! *Oh no, Lord. Haven't I been through enough?* I whined as I surveyed the human wreckage in the place which was to be my home for three months. *You changed my life forever in a split-second. Do You have to rub my nose in it by making me live in this depressing environment? Will my rehabilitation be as hideous and painful as it appears to be for these other patients? Am I going to end up with one of those halos screwed into my head?* I assured my parents as they settled me into my new environment that I was going to be fine, but inside I ached with anxiety and a gnawing sense of hopelessness.

In the middle of my second night at Craig I was startled awake by excruciating chest pains and I could hardly breathe. *I'm having a heart attack! My lung is collapsing! I'm dying!* my brain reacted in panic. Every attempted breath was painfully challenged by a knifelike jab inside my chest. My groans of pain alerted the nurse, who summoned the doctors. The doctors discovered the presence of a blood clot the size of a baseball in my lung. For two weeks I was confined to my bed on a steady diet of intravenous blood thinners and painkillers waiting for the clot to slowly dissolve. During this time I could take only very short breaths and each breath sent a shock of pain through my chest.

One night the pain in my chest was so intense I could hardly bear it. I had taken all the painkillers I was allowed and I still couldn't get to sleep. I groaned a prayer in the darkness of my room, "Lord, it hurts! Please help me!" Suddenly a tender scene from my childhood drifted through my curtain of pain to the forefront of my mind. I remembered my grandmother coming into my room at bedtime and sitting on my bed, as she did often when she visited us. Before kissing me good night, Grandma would coach me in reciting Bible verses. Often the tranquillity of Grandma's warm presence and soothing voice would send me floating off to sleep in the middle of a psalm I was trying to quote. Grandma's many visits during my childhood resulted in the formation of an extensive card file of Scripture in my memory. The older I became, the less "cool" I thought it was to have bedtime devotions with her. When she came to visit, I would either go to bed early or fake that I was already asleep when she came into my room.

But her spiritual input into my life during my formative years unexpectedly resurfaced that painful night in Craig Hospital. Many of the verses Grandma taught me came flooding back into my mind as I struggled against my pain. I began to recite them—in short, labored breaths—just as I had recited them to my grandmother. Miraculously, as I quoted the Scripture verses which came to mind, the pain subsided and I drifted off to sleep, pillowed on God's peace. Through that experience I heard the still, small voice of the Lord permeating the clatter of my pain, my fear, and my apprehension for the future: "I'm here, Randy, and I care about what's happening to you." It was an assurance I would need to hear many times in the months ahead.

During those first few weeks the doctors discovered that the incision on my neck had not healed properly. It gaped open, exposing my spine. One day my doctor announced, "We're going to close the incision surgically, Randy. Then we're going to put you in a halo to stabilize your neck." A sickening dread immediately knotted my stomach. The thought of having four holes drilled into my skull terrified me.

Again my mother's faith rose to the occasion. "We believe in the healing power of the Lord," she announced confidently to the doctors. "Randy will not need more surgery." My family and friends started praying for a miraculous healing of my neck. The neurosurgeon agreed to wait two weeks, but he insisted on surgery if the problem was not remedied in that time. Mom's confidence in God's ability inspired me. As the days crawled by, my faith began to grow. I knew that the Lord *could* heal me and that He *would* heal me. Mom and I huddled together daily to pray, and by the end of two weeks the incision had closed. No surgery—and no halo—was ever needed.

Near the end of my first month at Craig I was well enough to begin rehabilitative therapy. The first step in the process was a get-acquainted session with what was to become my constant companion as a quadriplegic: my wheelchair. Up until that time I rode around in a reclining tail-back chair because I wasn't strong enough to sit upright in a regular wheelchair. As the therapist assisted me into my chair for the first time, I was grateful for the temporary convenience it would provide me. But I wasn't ready to admit that the wheelchair would permanently take the place of my legs.

The medical staff assigned to my case—doctors, nurses, and therapists—scheduled a family conference to explain the goals and procedures of my rehabilitation. Mom was with me for the conference while Dad attended to business in Wichita. As she rolled me into the conference room, I was still hoping that one of the specialists would say, "Randy, due to some recent advances in technology, we'll have you back on your feet again as good as new in a couple of months." At the same time I trembled inside because I really didn't know what to expect in the weeks ahead at Craig, and I feared the sobering prospect of a lifetime in a wheelchair. The doctors displayed my X-rays on an illuminated wall screen in the conference room and explained in detail the physical consequences of my collision with the bottom of a mudhole.

We learned that when a break occurs in any one of the seven cervical vertebrae, with resulting damage to the related spinal nerves, the victim will be a quadriplegic with significant to total loss of movement in arms and legs. The higher the break, the more extensive will be the paralysis. Though some quads are able to learn to walk with braces, most are confined to wheelchairs.

If the damage to the spinal cord is in the low region of the cervical vertebrae (C-6 to C-8), the victim is known as a "super quad," retaining some or most of the functions of hands and arms. A C-8 quad has relatively good use of hands and arms. A C-7 loses some hand functions, but retains the use of biceps, triceps, elbows, and wrists. A C-6 is unable to use triceps and loses some function of the elbows, but retains control of biceps and radial wrist extensors. After rehabilitation, super quads usually require very little physical assistance.

The difference between a C-6 and a C-5 quad is significant. Damage in the C-5 region of the neck drastically limits the use of wrists and arms. The victim of a C-5 or above injury can do very little for himself. Damage at C-4 also includes paralysis of the shoulders. And if the break is in one of the three upper vertebrae (C-1 to C-3), the phrenic nerve is also damaged. The victim is a respiratory quadriplegic, almost totally paralyzed and unable to breathe without mechanical assistance.

Paraplegics are those whose spinal cord injuries occur below the cervical vertebrae, either in one of the 12 thoracic vertebrae behind the chest or one of the lumbar vertebrae of the lower back. Paraplegics generally have full use of their upper bodies. The higher the damage on the paraplegic's spinal cord, the more extensive the paralysis to the lower body.

The doctor touched his finger to a point on my X-ray which revealed the break in my neck. "Randy, your break categorizes you as a C-6 super quad."

A C-6 super quad, I thought dismally. *Sounds like some kind of a robot or half-human bionic man*. Something within me resisted such a dehumanizing title.

"After extensive physical therapy," the doctor continued, "you will regain a significant amount of strength and mobility in your arms and wrists, and a limited amount of the use of your hands."

I glanced at the two awkward-looking arms resting limply in my lap. They were my arms, but they didn't seem to be attached to me. They were no longer the skilled, muscular arms which lofted touchdown passes or launched 20-foot jump shots on the basketball court. They were skinny, pale, and weak. I could barely lift them to touch my face. My hands looked to be in even worse shape. The fingers were awkwardly curled from partial paralysis. It was hard to believe the doctor's claim that future use of these limbs could be termed "significant."

The doctor explained that the goal of the hospital was to teach the victims of spinal cord injuries a new way of life and to motivate them to get back into the mainstream by regaining as much use of their bodies as possible. They promised to provide whatever training, equipment, and psychological counseling necessary to help me return to the highest possible degree of normal living. They assured us that helping patients cope with depression, grief, anger, hostility, resistance, and adapting to their dependence on others is the responsibility not only of psychologists and counselors, but the entire staff. All of this was to be accomplished in an informal atmosphere, more like a college dormitory or a classroom than a hospital.

It was a great sales pitch, but I was waiting for the bottom line: walking. I wanted to hear them tell me about the miracles they were going to perform to get me back on my feet. The doctor must have sensed my anxiety. Finally he said, "Randy, the degree of your independence as a quad is directly related to the position of the broken vertebra. When the spinal cord is damaged at the C-6 level, the brain's message through the central nervous system telling the legs to walk is irreparably cut off. We're not going to tell you that you will never walk again, but the statistics behind your kind of injury offer virtually no hope. We're committed to helping you get the most out of what you have left. Unfortunately, your legs won't be part of the package."

Though I had expected them, the doctor's words were chilling. For the first time since my accident, the seriousness and finality of my injury hit me full force. The doctor's statement had quickly snuffed out the last flicker of hope for a medical miracle. It was like the clock had run out on me, my last-second shot for a winning basket had bounced off the rim, and the game was lost. It feels horrible to lose a game, but it was devastating to realize that I had lost the use of my legs and was confined to a wheelchair for the rest of my life. A sense of helplessness and a fear of the future swept over me like dark, angry waves threatening to drown me. I felt like I was at the bottom of that mudhole again—trapped, unable to move, unable to help myself.

Mom wheeled me out of the conference room and into the beautiful courtyard of the hospital. She sat down beside me in silence and tilted my head back on her shoulder. Suddenly the weight of my condition surged against my soul like a river at flood stage against a weakened dam. I crumbled inside and bawled like a baby. After several minutes of weeping, I felt Mom's steady faith again begin to radiate its light and warmth. "It's okay, Honey," she encouraged, wiping the tears from my eyes. "It's dark and ugly now, but we don't know what the Lord has for you yet. Let's look for His will and purpose in all this." Her words were right, but my feelings clawed at them as if God's will were my enemy.

Like so many Christians in the midst of trials and struggles, I didn't like the doctor's difficult answer to my problem. I wanted an easy answer and a quick fix. Life was supposed to be fun, not hard and painful. Christians were supposed to have the smoothest, most prosperous, and most successful lives of all. Up until the obstacle course on Lookout Mountain, I always *did* find the easy way out. Whenever pressures, problems, or pain crowded me, I either outmuscled them with my natural abilities or outran them through avoidance. I rarely needed God's help because I rarely allowed myself to get that uncomfortable. I had steadfastly pursued the good life, and anything which threatened to crimp my life-style was quickly conquered or completely avoided.

Now I was really stuck. I couldn't outmuscle or outrun my injury. Apart from a contemporary replay of the healing of the paralytic in Mark 2 (which I believe in and still pray for), I was going to be a quadriplegic for life. No more jogging in the woods. No more tennis matches. No more pickup basketball games or Sunday afternoon touch football games. Instead, everything would be a chore, including simple tasks such as shaving, brushing my teeth, putting on a pair of socks, or getting into the car. My lifelong, idealistic bubble of the easy Christian life had abruptly and painfully exploded.

One of the first things God taught me through my accident and rehabilitation was that I had been dead wrong about the Christian life. For 24 years I had bought into the misconception of Christianity which is shared by most of our society. People believe that once we say yes to the Lord and invite Him into our hearts, everything is going to be fine. Life will be comfortable, there will be no problems, and we will live in peace and happiness for the rest of our lives.

The problem with this great-sounding theory is that the Bible doesn't support it. God never promised Christians that life would be wonderful or easy, like the proverbial bowl of cherries. Rather, God has promised us quite the opposite. As I read the Bible and apply its principles to my life, one of the messages which comes through loudly and clearly is that Christians are called to suffer. As long as we live in a fallen world, we will experience pain, suffering, and struggles. Contrary to popular opinion, we don't receive an exemption from problems just because we are Christians. God causes the rain to fall on the just as well as on the unjust—that's just part of the game.

It's not our *susceptibility* to struggles, but our *response* to struggles that sets Christians apart from non-Christians. The "normal" response to problems and pain is to complain, to feel broken and defeated, to think you can't go on, to want to quit, and to ask, "Why me, Lord?" I was an expert in all those feelings even before I reached Craig Hospital. But I began realizing that, even though I suffered like everyone else in the world, I was not called to respond to suffering like the world does. God was reminding me that I enjoyed tremendous advantages as a Christian for responding positively to suffering. I had all the resources of my heavenly Father at my disposal through prayer. I had God's promise never to leave me or forsake me; He would be with me in my struggles. And if I learned to look at my injury through God's eyes, I would have a radically different perspective on the value of trials and struggles in my life. They are not the deliberate hurtful acts of a sadistic god who delights in making my life miserable. My problems, large and small, are the ordinary obstacles of human existence which God allows in my life to help me grow and develop godly character. God was challenging me to look at my injury through James' eyes: "When all kinds of trials and temptations crowd into your lives, my brothers, don't resent them as intruders, but welcome them as friends!" (James 1:2, PHILLIPS).

That's how Christians turn the tables on their struggles. Instead of letting them beat us, we beat them by using them as stepping-stones to growth. Instead of meeting them with our own strength and failing, we meet them with the strength that God gives and succeed. Instead of cowering in self-pity whining, "Why me?" we stand tall and march forward asking, "Where do we go from here?"

In those early days at Craig Hospital, Scriptures about being an overcomer and leading a victorious Christian life, which I had heard since boyhood, began to penetrate my consciousness. God seemed to be asking me, "If you always enjoy the easy life and never have any problems or struggles, what do you have to overcome? How can you be a victorious Christian if you never get into the battle?" I don't believe that God dragged me up to Lookout Mountain and forced me to run the obstacle course in order to shatter my comfort zone. It was my idea to accept the challenge to run the course. It was my foolish decision to dive into the mudhole. Even though God didn't cause my accident, it was no surprise to Him—He watched it happen. As I began my strenuous rehabilitation program at Craig, He seemed to say to me, "Randy, I know your accident was a tragedy to you. But I'm with you. If you let Me, I will help you rise above your unpleasant circumstance to become a real overcomer." It was an offer I tearfully resisted on a number of occasions, but which I couldn't ultimately refuse.

The importance of welcoming Christ into my struggle and becoming an overcomer was brought home to me forcefully through a Christian friend of mine from Wichita named Brian Linn. Brian was a great athlete and a tremendous amateur golfer. One evening during my rehab at Craig, another friend from Wichita called with some news about Brian.

"Brian is trying out for the pro tour," Brad reported.

"That's great!" I replied, always happy to hear about another athlete succeeding.

"But there's some bad news too," Brad continued. "Brian's been having stomach problems, so they put him in the hospital. Today they cut him open, and he was so full of cancer they could do nothing but sew him up. He has about three months to live."

I was stunned as I hung up the phone. "Forgive me, Lord," I prayed. "Here I am feeling sorry for myself because of my injury, when my friend Brian is lying in a hospital bed with only three months to live."

Weeks later after I returned to Wichita, Brian and I attended a Bible study together. We were quite a pair. I was still clumsily learning how to live in a wheelchair, and Brian was in such pain that it took him several minutes to walk across a room. We shared a lot of hurt and pain together during his last precious weeks. We could empathize with each other as few people could. When he died it was as if I had lost one of only a handful of people in the world who spoke my language. He understood the inner pain I struggled against like few people I have known.

During our weeks of suffering and tears together, Brian and I came to a very important, mutual decision. Our decision was far from a panacea for our physical pain and limitations or the emotional anguish which accompanied them, but it was a tiny ark of temporary shelter amidst the flood of negative feelings and questions which battered us mercilessly. Whenever one of us was down, the other would remind him of our mutual commitment: Even in the midst of our struggles and pain, we would rather have Jesus Christ than to trade places with anybody else and not have Him. Brian died within six months of being diagnosed with cancer.

Whenever the suffering I experience clouds the simple answers I seek, I hear my soul brother Brian Linn encouraging me, "Live for Jesus; that's all that matters." It was something I would need to hear often.

4
Full Speed Ahead

//

Up until my accident I had been deeply involved in athletics most of my life. During junior high and high school I participated in two, three, and even four inter-scholastic sports a year. Every sport I played required hours of physical conditioning, skill development, train-ing, and practice. Competing in the actual game was the glory part of the sport, but it was only the tip of the iceberg for me as an athlete. Behind every contest were countless hours of monotonous exercises and drills which pushed my strength and endurance to the limit. During college I limited my participation to basketball and then tennis, but the physical and mental preparation for intercollegiate competition was still demanding. Even after college I continued a strenuous plan of daily condi-tioning right up to the day of my accident.

I have never been a stranger to hard work in the weight room or on the practice field. I have always risen to the physical challenge of being the best I can be. But all my years of conditioning and training for sports were child's play compared to the toilsome routine and the grueling schedule of my rehab at Craig Hospital. The hospital staff was dead serious in their commitment to help me regain the highest possible degree of normal living. They squeezed blood, sweat, and tears out of me every day for about two-and-a-half months to fulfill their commitment. I have never worked so hard or so long to achieve what seemed so little change in my life.

My days at Craig started at 6:00 A.M., and it was nonstop work, work, work, push, push, push until about 4:30 P.M. My daily regimen involved two kinds of therapy—physical and occupational. The goals of physical therapy were to help me recover maximum usage of the muscles I still controlled and maintain good cardiovascular circulation in the paralyzed muscles. Every day I spent hours in the therapy pool and the gym pushing and pulling, stretching and straining as my slave-driving therapists demanded: "Do it again, Randy"; "Push harder, Randy"; "Stretch farther, Randy."

One of the most important physical skills I had to master was transfers—moving myself from the wheelchair to a standard chair and back again, from the wheelchair to the bed and back again, from the wheelchair to the car and back again, etc. The staff was not about to break their backs lifting full-grown quads like me from place to place. Their top priority was to build up my arm muscles so I could get myself in and out of bed. I worked on transfers until I was blue in the face.

Occupational therapy was aimed at helping me learn to perform daily living tasks, such as dressing, grooming, and getting around in a wheelchair, within the limitations of my paralyzed legs and partially paralyzed arms and hands. Essentially I had to relearn every simple task which my body had forgotten because of my injury. It was like being in kindergarten again—this time as an adult. I had to retrain my muscles all over again to use such implements as a toothbrush, comb, and eating utensils.

I also had to attend dressing class and learn how to dress myself. The coordination in my arms and hands was pretty bad, so it took forever to accomplish tasks which only took me seconds to complete before my accident. One morning my project in dressing class was learning to put on my socks. I started at about nine o'clock with one sock. "Sue, this is impossible," I griped to my therapist after my first few attempts. "My crazy fingers can't even hold the sock, let alone get it over my toes."

"You've got to keep working on it, Randy," Sue insisted unsympathetically. "You've got to make your muscles perform, and that's going to take time. Keep trying." She walked away to encourage someone else. I gritted my teeth and determinedly guided my uncooperative hands to pick up the sock again.

After about an hour I had inched my sock halfway over my foot. A half-hour later the sock was barely over my heel, and in another half-hour I had reached my ankle. By about 11:30 A.M. my sock was completely on. I was elated and called my therapist over so I could show off. "Look, Sue. I did it!" I boasted proudly.

Sue looked down at my foot with a smile of approval. "Yes, Randy, that's great." Then she yanked my sock off, tossed it into my lap, and said as she walked away, "Now do it again." I was so deflated and angry that I could have shot her on the spot. But that was the nature of the therapy at Craig—pushing patients hard and long to help them recover as much ability as possible. My therapists at Craig were the most demanding, relentless coaches I have ever trained under. They pushed me to the absolute maximum.

I also learned that receiving occupational therapy could be dangerous, and sometimes even entertaining. One day in dressing class I was learning to put on my pants. My therapist told me to sit on the side of the bed, rock gently side to side, and tug up my jeans inch by inch until I had them over my hips. As usual, I approached the task with a vengeance. During one enthusiastic attempt I got to rocking a little too vigorously. I lost my balance, tumbled helplessly backwards off the bed, and landed in a heap on the floor. When I realized that I wasn't hurt, I started to giggle and soon I was laughing almost hysterically. The therapists and other patients huddled around me with concern, thinking I had hurt myself. I was laughing so hard I couldn't speak. I was seeing a mental snapshot of myself which just cracked me up. There I was crumpled on the floor in my underwear with my elbows and knees pointed every which way and my jeans tangled around my ankles. The memory of my first slapstick attempt at getting into jeans kept me entertained for months.

On the serious side, that first episode with my sock brought me face-to-face with my greatest opponent during my arduous rehabilitation: the temptation to give up. There were lots of days when the taxing routine seemed like too much. I didn't want to work out or go swimming. I didn't want to sit for 45 minutes trying to button my shirt or spend half an hour smearing toothpaste all over my face as I attempted to brush my teeth. The most fundamental tasks were herculean undertakings for me. I had to work so hard and so long just to accomplish what able-bodied people could do almost subconsciously. In my darker moments I wondered, *What's the use? What do I really have to live for? My body is a mess and my dreams are shattered. I may someday learn to dress myself, to drive, and maybe even to walk with braces. But I'm still a cripple, and I'll never play ball or coach again.* Some days I just wanted to stay in bed and not hassle with the tedium of transfers, dressing, and grooming.

I was no stranger to feelings of wanting to quit. As a boy growing up, there were many times in sports when I wanted to give up. Some of them are laughable now, but the disappointment and discouragement I faced were very real at the time. One of the first times I wanted to hang it up was when I played seventh-grade basketball. I was really excited about making the seventh-grade basketball team until I realized that *everybody* made the seventh-grade basketball team. When the coach passed out uniforms, I couldn't wait to get home and try mine on. I excitedly pulled on my shorts and jersey, then stepped in front of the full-length mirror. I was horrified at what I saw. I gave out such a shrill scream that my mother came running up the stairs shouting, "Randy, what's the matter?"

I said, "Mom, look at these shorts! I can parachute in these shorts!" I had scrawny little bird-legs and my uniform shorts were so big that I was sure I could jump out my second-story window and parachute safely to the ground. "If you think for one minute I'm going to run out on the basketball court and let the girls see me in these shorts, you're crazy! If you don't take them in, I'm not showing up tomorrow." I was ready to pack it in on my basketball career right then and there. Lucky for me, Mom was great about calming my childish fears and taking in my basketball shorts.

The next year I got involved in eighth-grade football. When our team first started practicing, we really pounded on each other. We thought we were real tough—and we *were* tough for a team of little guys. But our first game was against a team of big guys and we got beat, 42-0. That was only the beginning. The year turned out to be one of the most traumatic in my athletic career. Our team was 0-8. We only scored four touchdowns all season, and two of those came in the same game when we were losing so badly that our opponents' coach sent in his second-string defense against us.

I was so humiliated by the end of the season that I decided to quit football for good—but my dad had different ideas. Collegiate High School is a small four-year school and our teams needed all the bodies they could recruit. Dad felt the smallness of Collegiate offered me a great opportunity to play high school football. I was a five-foot eight-inch, 113-pound wimp, but my dad said, "You're going to play football. It will make a man out of you." And when your dad is also the school's headmaster, you better plan on doing what he says!

So the next year I went out for the varsity football team as a freshman and became the second-string quarterback. I was glad to be second-string because I didn't particularly want to play. Before every game I prayed for the safety of our quarterback so I wouldn't have to go into the game.

About the third week of the season the coach called me into his office. I walked in with a smile on my face and hoping he was going to suggest that football wasn't my sport. Instead he put his arm around my shoulder and said, "Randy, you're going to be our starting quarterback this week." I was speechless—not from excitement, but from fear. "Our first-string quarterback is also our best running back," he continued. "All you have to do is take the snap from center and hand the ball off to him."

It didn't sound too difficult to me, so I was relieved. Then I learned that our opponent in the next game was ranked third in the state. I was a wreck during that week of practice. I was nervous on Monday, *really* nervous on Tuesday, paranoid on Wednesday, didn't know my name on Thursday, and on Friday I told my mom I was sick and couldn't go to school. But my wise mom knew better, and she dropped me off as usual.

That night my stomach was in my throat as our team arrived at the stadium, got suited up and taped up, and trotted onto the field. We received the kickoff and the coach sent me in with the first play—a 333 trap. It was an easy play; I'd run it hundreds of times in practice. All I had to do was take the snap from the center, turn around, fake to the fullback, and give the ball to our tailback. But when we broke the huddle and came up to the line of scrimmage, I almost passed out. The guys on the other side of the line were huge. Their uniforms were red and white, and they looked like the Nebraska Cornhuskers.

I got under the center and started calling the signals. But an instant before the center snapped the ball, I stepped back to avoid getting creamed by the defense. The ball bounced between my legs, the other team recovered it, and before the game was one minute old we were down 7-0.

We received the second kickoff and the coach called the same play. When I came up behind the center to call the signals, their lineman looked even bigger. In my fear I again pulled away from the center too soon. The ball bounced wildly into our backfield, the other team recovered again, and before the game was three minutes old we were behind 14-0. When I came off the field, the fans for the other team gave me a standing ovation as the best player on their team. I knew the coach was going to send me to the showers, but he grabbed me by the face mask and said, "Calm down, Randy. I'm going to put you in there one more time."

The big guys kicked off for the third time and the coach sent me in with the 333 trap again. When I went up to the line of scrimmage I told myself that I had to stay under the center until the ball was snapped. I barked out the signals and the center slapped the ball into my hands. But instead of turning to hand it off, I stood frozen in my tracks and was buried by a wave of red-and-white-clad monsters. The ball popped loose and was recovered by the defense, and before the game was five minutes old we were behind 21-0. I didn't play the rest of the game. I was completely humiliated and ready to quit football again.

Later that night Dad and I sat at the kitchen table eating pie as I tried to convince him to let me give up football. I was so embarrassed by my performance that I didn't want to show up at school on Monday morning.

"It was just a bad game, Randy," Dad encouraged warmly. "Joe Namath had his share of fumbles and interceptions, but he kept going. If you give up now, you'll never know how much better you can get." Once again Dad's encouragement saved the day. I survived my freshman season and went on to a great sophomore season playing alongside my friend Jack Chesky.

These times of embarrassment on the prep school court and field were relatively minor temptations to give up. I chuckle about them now. But I also suffered some hurtful experiences outside of sports during my college days which weren't funny at all. The temptation to give up in these situations was even stronger. One of the most painful of these occurred when I was a sophomore at William Jewell College in Missouri. I'd been dating a Wichita girl since the middle of high school. She was a wonderful girl, and I was sure she was the one for me. I just knew I was going to marry her someday.

I came home from college one weekend and we went out on a date as we usually did. Something about my girlfriend's behavior that night didn't seem quite right to me, but I was in love so it didn't really bother me much. When I walked her to the door at the end of the evening, she said, "Randy, there's something I need to talk to you about."

I said, "Sure, what is it? You can tell me anything."

She looked at the ground and nervously twirled her hair. "I know this may come as a shock to you," she said haltingly. "But I won't be going out with you anymore."

I was stunned. I couldn't believe what I had heard. "Why? What's wrong? What have I done?" I stammered defensively.

"It's nothing you have done," she said. "I've just realized that I don't love you anymore."

I tried to explain my feelings for her, but her mind was made up. We said our final painful good-byes, then she walked inside and closed the door on me forever. I stumbled to the car and drove home in a daze. For the first time in my life I had been deeply hurt in a relation-ship. The girl I wanted to marry had turned me out of her life. Suddenly nothing else in life was important to me—college, sports, success. Everything seemed worthless without her. For the next several weeks I just wanted to crawl into a hole and give up.

During my rehab at Craig some of those same dark feelings of wanting to give up moved in on me again, but this time these feelings were infinitely more intense. It would have been so easy to give up. My glorious athletic past was history, my present circumstances were humiliating and painful, and my future looked hopeless. Self-pity kept whispering its depressing message in my ear: "You've broken your neck and it will never be fixed. You're finished. Don't fight it. All you have to look forward to is going home to Wichita and waiting out the rest of your life in a wheelchair."

Ironically, the same thing which saved my life physically also saved my life emotionally: athletics. If I had not been in such good physical condition at the time of my accident, I would have never lived to see Craig Hospital. And if I had not been ingrained with the never-give-up approach to life which I learned through athletics, I never would have survived the rigors and disappointments of rehabilitation.

During my first few weeks in Denver I began to realize that my years in sports were a great training ground for dealing with the emotional trauma of my injury. I thought about the one basic rule of competitive sports which was continually drilled into me as an athlete: Don't ever quit. I heard it in pregame, halftime, and postgame pep talks from the first time I put on a uniform: "It doesn't matter what the score is, how tough the situation is, how big the opponents are, or how dim the future looks. Winners never quit and quitters never win. Dig in, suck it up, hang tough." I'd been told that the true greatness of an athlete is measured by the size of the challenge it takes to knock him down. No player needs to be ashamed of playing his best, giving 100 percent, and hanging in there even in a losing effort. But pity the poor athlete who gives up on a play, on his teammates, or on the game when he is losing—especially if he must face a coach like some of the ones I played for!

As a patient at Craig I began to see that the discipline of hanging tough in difficult circumstances was a principle for my life as well as for my past in sports. Up until my injury, my life had been a series of successes, much like my high school sports history. Suddenly I was up against the biggest opponent I had ever faced, and my circumstances had ground me into the turf. I was now an underdog in life—a quadriplegic in a world which acclaims the body beautiful and often shuns the handicapped. I was faced with the challenge of playing the rest of the game of life injured. I could either feel sorry for myself and take myself out of the game by giving up on life, or I could suck it up and go for it against all odds.

Three young men at Craig—fellow patients of mine named Tim, Angelo, and Walt—graphically illustrated to me the contrast between quitters and overcomers. Tim was one of my first roommates at Craig. He was a high school boy who had broken his neck playing football. Tim had been a patient at Craig Hospital for six months before I arrived, but he hadn't made any progress in rehab because he had literally given up on life and given up on himself. He wouldn't get out of bed in the morning or go to therapy. When anyone tried to push him along, Tim would just whine and cry. His dad would call him on the phone to encourage him and Tim would end up in tears of self-pity. His mom would come to the hospital and try to work with him, but he refused her help. He had given up and there was no helping him. The last thing I heard about Tim, he was sitting at home doing nothing but feeling sorry for himself. He didn't think he had anything left to live for, so he gave up. He was the pathetic example of the quitter my coaches loathed. I could identify perfectly with Tim's attitude because I had the same temptation to give up. I knew the hopeless, empty feeling of being an athlete who would never play again. But I also knew that giving up would violate everything I had ever been taught about sports and life. Tim's negative example spurred me on to overcome my injury and stay in the game.

Angelo, a 14-year-old fellow patient from Texas, had been injured in a bizarre incident on a dirt bike. Angelo and his friend were riding the dirt bike on his friend's property. The man who lived on the adjoining property was a little crazy, and in a fit of insane rage he came after the boys with a double-barreled shotgun. One blast killed Angelo's friend and the other hit Angelo in the back of the neck, totally paralyzing him from the neck down. Angelo had every reason to be bitter about losing the use of his arms and legs before he ever learned to drive a car. But Angelo wasn't like Tim.

"Hey, Randy, how are you doing?" Angelo greeted me cheerily one day when I was feeling a little sorry for myself.

"What does it matter how I'm doing?" I snapped at him. "Every day is the same as the last. Work, sweat, and strain—but we don't improve enough to make a difference."

"Don't talk like that, Randy," he admonished. "We *are* gaining. Little by little I'm getting the hang of my motorized wheelchair. And I can see you improve a little every day too. Don't give up. You've got a great future ahead of you."

Angelo was in worse shape than I was, but what a positive attitude he had! He was working hard to make the best of his bad situation. Angelo is a fighter and a winner, and he's not going to give up. He's going to make it.

Walt was one of my next-door neighbors in the hospital. Before coming to Craig, Walt was diagnosed with leukemia, and his doctors prescribed treatment with chemotherapy. But a tragic reaction to the chemotherapy left Walt paralyzed, so he was transferred to Craig for rehabilitation while still suffering from leukemia. Walt's pain was so great that he had to take morphine, and he became addicted to it. If anybody had a reason to give up on life, it was Walt. Instead he was always looking on the bright side of things. He was a real inspiration to me.

One day I had a terribly difficult time in therapy. I came back to my room exhausted and deeply discouraged. I just wanted to shut the door and go to bed. I didn't want to have anything to do with rehabilitation. "What's it for?" I grumbled as I transferred into bed and pulled up the covers. "I'm going to be this way for the rest of my life. Why in the world should I get up and try to make something out of myself when there's nothing left to work with?" I was in the pits and ready to throw in the towel.

All of a sudden someone knocked on my door and, before I could hide under the covers, in rolled my friend Walt. He began telling me how thankful he was to be going home in a few days. "I have a wonderful wife who has been very supportive. And my job is still waiting for me at home. I can't wait to get back into the groove."

I felt so ashamed. Here was a guy battling paralysis and morphine addiction, who would probably die from leukemia in a few years, telling me how thankful he was! He wasn't groveling in self-pity or giving up. Instead he was determined to make the best out of his bad situation. I doubt that he's still alive today, but Walt was one of the most positive, uplifting guys I've ever been around.

So much of our success in our circumstances has to do with attitude. As I reflected on the positive attitudes displayed by guys like Walt and Angelo, I knew I couldn't take the easy way out and give up. I realized that the Lord was on my team and that He gives us the courage and strength to stand up under the stiffest test. After all, I reasoned, if God can't make the best out of a bad situation, He isn't God. Every time I came across quitters like Tim at Craig, I winced at my own tendencies to give up which I saw reflected in them. But, thankfully, I ran into overcomers like Angelo and Walt who steadily firmed my resolve not to let my handicap beat me. That attitude continues to make all the difference in my life today.

As I look around me today, I see a lot of people like Tim who are giving up on life, giving up on their families, giving up on their dreams, giving up on their friends, giving up on themselves, and giving up on God. We're a very selfish and apathetic society. When things don't go our way, our first reaction is to slough it off and do something else. We look for the path of least resistance. We don't want to stick with anything that requires tenacity and perseverance over the long haul. We don't want to pay the price of hard work which is often necessary if we're going to make the grade. Instead of toughing it out when life gets hard, our society is taking the easy way out through alcohol, drugs, illicit sex, and divorce. People are trying to find someone or something which will smother the pain with pleasure, even if it's only temporary. Many of the high school kids I work with today are trying to find a way out of painful home situations and social relationships. They are—as the song says—looking for love in all the wrong places. Our only hope in the struggles of our lives is not to give up and walk away, but to take the hand of Christ and battle through the problems.

A couple of years ago I spoke at a Fellowship of Christian Athletes' retreat in Rock Springs, Kansas. I shared my testimony and challenged the young men and women in the audience not to give up in their struggles, but to commit their lives to Christ and hang in there. At the end of the evening a beautiful 17-year-old girl asked if she could talk to me. Tears began streaming down her cheeks as she said, ''Randy, my life is so messed up and I don't know where to turn. A few weeks ago I gave birth to a six-pound baby boy and had to put him up for adoption. I got pregnant with him because two years ago I had an abortion. I know it sounds crazy, but I felt so guilty about destroying a human life that I had to bring another life into the world. Now I feel terrible about losing my son. Besides, my mom has been married four times and our relationship is a mess. And I never see my dad. I'm about ready to give up."

I had the great privilege of sharing the Lord with her that night. I told her that Christ would make a difference in her life. He would help her put her life back together, and He would help her get through the tough stuff still ahead. The next morning during the service she walked forward and received Christ into her heart. She went home a different person, and the following spring she brought 25 young people from her school to the retreat. Jesus Christ had transformed her from a potential quitter to an overcomer.

That was the key I discovered as I wrestled through the depression of my first weeks at Craig: acknowledging that Jesus Christ was right in the middle of my struggle with me. My greatest temptation was to focus on my problem and my depressing future, but I began to see that a faulty focus like that was a sure way to becoming a quitter like Tim. Instead, if I began to seek Him and His kingdom first even when I felt like quitting, everything I needed to handle my problem would be provided. Yes, things were still difficult and I still felt like giving up at times. But I knew the only way out of my situation was to grab hold of Jesus and rise above it.

One of my favorite movies is *Rocky IV*. When Rocky Balboa was getting ready to fight the big Russian, Rocky's son pleaded with him not to do it. He said something like, "Dad, he's so big, he's so strong. He kills. He killed your friend Apollo Creed."

But Rocky's response was the classic response for someone battling the temptation to give up. It summarizes the attitude of a winner, whether the obstacle is a physical injury, an illness, a family problem, a job problem, or whatever: "Going one more round when you don't think you can, that's what living is all about." In those tough early days at Craig Hospital, God kept drumming that Rocky spirit into me: "Going one more round with your therapy when you don't think you can, going one more round with your pain when you don't think you can, going one more round with your frustration and your discouragement when you don't think you can, that's what being an overcomer is all about."

5

No One Waits Out the Storm Alone

//

In some ways, moving into Craig Hospital for rehabilitation was like being exiled to a foreign country. I was hundreds of miles away from the comfortable, familiar surroundings of Wichita and Chattanooga. My fellow patients at the hospital—victims of spinal cord and brain injuries or illnesses—were like another race of people I had never been exposed to. By reason of my injury, I was a full-fledged citizen; I was one of them. I had to learn their methods of dealing with everyday life. I had to learn the language of our common disability. The net emotional effect on me was a sense of loneliness and isolation from the life I had so abruptly left behind. I felt afraid, lost, and alone in the upside-down world of paraplegics and quadriplegics.

But early in my three-month rehabilitation ordeal, God made it apparent to me that He hadn't lost track of me. He knew exactly where I was and how I felt. He made it very clear to me that He understood my fear and pain and that He was committed to loving me in the midst of my uncomfortable new environment. The primary way by which He invaded my loneliness and fear with His love was through people. God marched a number of people into my life to help me make the transition to life as a quad.

One of the earliest evidences of His love literally burst in on me during my first week at Craig while I was suffering incredible pain from the blood clot in my lung. One day I was lying in bed half dopey from painkillers and feeling terrible. Suddenly there was a woman by the side of my bed. "Hi, Randy," she said cheerily. "My name is Ima Closter."

I was so "out of it" in my discomfort that I barely acknowledged she was there. I thought, *Lady, I don't know anybody named Ima Closter. What are you doing in my room?*

"We've never met, Randy," she continued, "but my cousin is your grandmother's mailman down in Troy, Tennessee." My interest in Ima rose slightly when she mentioned Troy, Tennessee, where my grandmother lived. "Your grandmother told my cousin, who is her mailman, all about your injury. She told him that you were being transferred from Chattanooga to Denver for treatment. When my cousin told me you were here, I thought I would come by and see if there was anything I could do for you."

The last thing I felt like doing at the moment was chat with my grandmother's mailman's cousin. So I mumbled something about needing a lot of prayer and hoped she would go away. She sensed my discomfort, offered a short but sincere prayer for me, and left, promising to come see me again.

And she did come back repeatedly. Ima Closter was a self-appointed committee of one who was determined to share God's love with me in the hospital. During my stay at Craig, Ima brought me a hot, home-cooked meal about once a week. She was a beautiful instrument of blessing whom the Lord prepared for me in Denver. Ima was a signpost of God's loving involvement with me in the uncomfortable hospital environment.

Another channel of God's blessing to me in Denver was Callie Vickers, one of my mom's dearest friends. Callie lived in Wichita before moving to Denver a couple of years before my accident. Mom stayed with her often during my months at Craig. Callie and her husband, Jack, visited me several times and were among the most faithful in praying for me during their visits. Shirley, a new friend who lived with Jack and Callie, brought me several helpings of her special, delicious barbecued chicken.

Another friend of my mom's in the Denver area, Elizabeth Miller, called me one day and asked, "Randy, I'd like to bring you a bunch of sweet peas. Would that be okay?"

"Sure, that would be nice," I answered weakly. At the time I didn't realize sweet peas were flowers; I thought Elizabeth was talking about bringing me a bowlful of garden peas to eat. I hate peas, but I didn't feel right about turning down her kindness. I dreaded the day when she would show up with sweet peas, because I just knew I would have to eat some of them in front of her and pretend to like them.

I was relieved when Elizabeth arrived with a lovely bouquet of flowers instead of a bowl of vegetables, and we had a good laugh when I admitted my ignorance. Elizabeth brought me a beautiful fresh bouquet of flowers every week during my stay at Craig. Each colorful arrangement was a visible, encouraging reminder that God had not abandoned me in Denver. He kept bringing people into my life—some I knew and some I didn't know—to demonstrate His love in specific ways.

The greatest evidence of God's love for me during rehab was in the person of the Christian roommate He brought me. Wayne Hazel was about five years older than I. He came to Craig Hospital for rehabilitation about two weeks after I did. Ironically, Wayne, who lived in Kingston Springs, Tennessee, broke his neck in a sports-related accident and was admitted to Erlanger Hospital in Chattanooga the day after I was. We were actually in the intensive care unit at Erlanger at the same time, but we were so sick and immobilized that we never met until he and I were assigned to a two-man room at Craig. Wayne's wife, Patsy, became acquainted with my parents in the waiting room at Erlanger, and it was Mom and Dad who persuaded the Hazels to consider treatment at Craig.

Wayne and I discovered that we shared many common interests such as sports and our faith in Christ, and we soon became fast friends. We worked hard together. My injury was a little worse than his, but our rehab was similar. Wayne and I enjoyed the friendly competition in our therapy which helped keep us both motivated. Wayne's lovely wife, Patsy, was with him each step of the way. During our three months together Wayne became a part of my family and I became a part of his.

Wayne and I literally shared everything with each other. If I picked up a virus or an infection, Wayne got it two days later. If he got it first, I got it from him. Because our injuries were so similar, Wayne and I could relate to each other's struggles and disappointments. We talked together, prayed together, shed many tears together, and understood each other like few people could. In the painful, stressful circumstances of rehabilitation we discovered a great beauty: We had each other. I saw in Wayne the familiar shadow of my friend Jack Chesky. Like Jack, Wayne became my brother, and our love for each other during those three months became a rock of stability for both of us. As a Christian, Wayne was a major influence in my life to strengthen me emotionally and spiritually. Together we hosted a weekly Bible study for our floor which was usually attended by three or four other patients.

Like most brothers, Wayne and I played hard together. Being young and a little cocky, Wayne and I seemed to inspire each other to mischief. After a couple of months together we practically ran the hospital. For instance, all the other patients dutifully wheeled themselves down to the cafeteria to eat meals. But we decided that we deserved better treatment, so we talked my mom and Patsy into providing us with room service—which they did! We were spoiled rotten.

Wayne and I devised another sneaky scheme while the World Series was being played that year. Normally all wheelchair patients had to attend wheelchair class every day. The object of the class was to build up our arm muscles by having us wheel ourselves all over the grounds of the hospital for a couple of hours each day. It was really boring, especially when we knew that the World Series was on TV.

"I don't want to go to wheelchair class today, Wayne," I announced to my roommate as we finished our lunch. "I want to relax and watch the World Series this afternoon. It's going to be a great game."

"I'm with you, Randy," Wayne said. "But you know the only way we will miss wheelchair class is if the therapists cancel it—and they'll never do it."

"Well, if they don't cancel class today," I replied as a solution popped into my head, "then somebody will have to cancel class for them."

Wayne laughed aloud, reading my mind, and we rolled into action. He began preparing our room for visitors, and I wheeled out into the hall to look for an unattended phone. I slyly cruised into an empty office, picked up a hospital phone, and punched in the code for the intercom. Patients were not supposed to know the code, but Wayne and I had figured it out! In my most official-sounding voice I announced to all the patients in their rooms: "Attention, please. Wheelchair class has been canceled today due to the World Series. There will be a meeting in Room 220 to watch today's game on television."

The entire class rolled into our room to watch the game. Meanwhile, the therapists couldn't figure out why nobody showed up for wheelchair class. They were furious when they finally found us eating popcorn, drinking Cokes, and enjoying the game. But we were having such a good time that they soon saw the humor of the situation and joined us to watch the rest of the game.

Wayne is one of many people in my life who have made a tremendous impact on me before and since my accident. I call them my heroes. These are the people who have modeled the true qualities of friendship—unconditional love, honesty, consistency, transparency, support. The heroes in my life confront me when I need it. My heroes selflessly reach beyond themselves to put others first. They don't waste time talking about doing things for others; they just do them. My heroes are the people I most want to emulate.

After my injury, when my need for people became vividly apparent to me, I began consciously recognizing and appreciating the people God had placed in my life to support me, love me, and direct me. I've had heroes around me all my life, but I didn't notice them until I had suffered my debilitating injury. That's when my heroes' true colors showed best, and that's when I began to appreciate their contributions to my life.

Right at the top of my list of heroes are my parents. When I was a child they surrounded me with acceptance. One or both of them attended every one of my games during high school, home or away. They were my greatest fans. Mom and Dad equipped me with the values which have carried me through my ordeal and serve as the foundation of my life today. They made sure I was in church on Sunday, and they filled our family times with Bible readings and prayers. They are still my principle spiritual mentors.

Mom is the greatest optimist in our family, always upbeat, always there. She's the glue that keeps our family together. Mom is the warmest, most loving, and most supportive person I've ever been around. When I was in high school, I'd come home Friday afternoons before a game and she'd have a steak and baked potato waiting for me. Those special steak dinners really boosted my morale and sent me off to the game feeling like a winner.

When I was away in college, Mom wrote me once a week, and she sent me delicious "care packages" during finals week. She's always had my best interest at heart and I love her for that. She's one of the finest Christian women I know.

If I could pattern my life after one man, I would choose to be like my dad. He has demonstrated to me through his life what it means to be honest, to treat people fairly, and to work hard. Being an athlete himself, Dad followed my sports career and encouraged me all the way, even kicking me in the backside when I needed it. So many afternoons as a boy I waited on the porch for him to come home from work so we could play catch. No matter how tired he was, Dad always set aside his briefcase to catch my passes or hit ground balls to me on the baseball field. I have been the recipient of his toughness both as his son and his student, and I'm grateful that he cared enough to shape me through discipline. I've also been the beneficiary of his loving heart which is as big as all the outdoors.

After my accident, my family was my greatest source of support and encouragement. Mom, Dad, and my sister, Melissa, stayed with me in Chattanooga for the whole month of my recovery. When I was transferred to Craig, Mom stayed with me in the hospital for a number of weeks. She learned how to bathe me, groom me, and dress me before I could do anything for myself. Dad and Melissa flew out to Denver whenever they could get away from their duties in Wichita. When I moved home, my family gave of themselves tirelessly to help me adjust to my new life in a wheelchair.

Melissa is a devoted, compassionate, and supportive sister, and I love her dearly. With my parents now living in Georgia, Melissa willingly drops whatever she's doing to give me a hand whenever I need it. Both of my grandmothers have been pillars of influence and support in my life through their prayers and encouragement. My family of heroes is the main reason why I couldn't give up in my discouraging battle with rehabilitation at Craig and afterward. They wouldn't let me give up. They accepted me as I was, but they refused to let me settle for mediocrity in my recovery.

As I work with high school kids today, I am saddened that many of them treat their parents as intrusions into their lives. There are many kids who have been blessed with parents like mine. I tell these kids that God's greatest gifts to them are their parents. They need to see their parents as heroes in their lives. There are other kids who don't have parents like mine. Sadly, these parents have chosen not to accept the responsibility to care for their kids as my parents have cared for me. I tell kids from these homes that God can still use their parents to help shape their lives if the kids will relate to their parents with respect.

My coach in high school, Coach Carter, is one of my heroes. He made a tremendous impact on my life during my teenage years. I played football, basketball, and track for him for three years. He is a great motivator and teacher, and a terrific competitor. Later he became an exemplary Christian witness in the world of sports. He contributed greatly to my sense of worth as a person and as an athlete. He generously praised me when I deserved it, and he thoroughly chewed me out when I needed it. He worked hard to pull out of me the best I could be. I consider Coach Carter partly responsible for saving my life. He instilled in me the physical toughness and never-give-up attitude which helped pull me through my injury and keep me going.

I have also found some true heroes among my friends. From the second grade on Lance Sandlian, Ron Innes, and I were very close. I was privileged to serve as best man at both of their weddings. The day after I was injured Lance dropped everything and hurried down to Chattanooga—so did another friend, Doug Leach. There was little they could do for me, but they just wanted to be there for me. On the day I arrived at Craig Hospital, Ernest Alexander, a dear friend from college, met me there. He was a singer on tour, but he took time out of his schedule to be with me at a very stressful time. Just seeing his friendly face at the hospital was a tremendous boost to my morale.

I celebrated my twenty-fifth birthday while at Craig Hospital, and a group of friends flew in for a very special birthday party. It blew my mind that people like Mark Dorian, Tracie Laham, Greg Ferris, and Brad and Jackie Lafever would travel such a distance for me. The devotion of my friends has helped me be a better friend.

I would have never made it through rehab if it hadn't been for my heroes at Craig Hospital, specifically my therapists Kathy Lyle and Sue Gordon. When I first met Kathy and Sue I didn't have a clue about what I was getting into under their care. They were both as loving, kind, and encouraging as they could be. They were also thoroughly professional in their approach, relentless in their persistence, and as tough as nails. They absolutely worked my tail off, and I really grew to love and appreciate them.

Kathy, my physical therapist, worked with me on muscle conditioning and transfers. I called her "Bulldog" for her tenacity at keeping me on task. Her goal was to help me regain as much physical strength and agility as possible through weight lifting, exercise, and swimming. Sue was my occupational therapist, and she helped me with tasks like dressing, daily hygiene, and grooming. Sue and her husband, Dave, also helped meet some of my spiritual needs. On Sundays they would come to the hospital, load me into their car, and take me to their church.

Kathy and Sue were God's instruments for equipping me physically, mentally, and emotionally for life as a quadriplegic. They inspired me to hard work, and I would work like a dog for them until I finished my tasks. Like other coaches who brought out the best in me, Kathy and Sue were willing to let me try anything I was willing to try. Their comment to me when I left the hospital was, "We have only one complaint: You expect too much out of yourself." To me that was a compliment. A lot of times my expectations for myself were probably unreasonable, but I would rather shoot high and not make it all the way to the top than to shoot low and not achieve my potential.

Another helpful member of the Craig Hospital staff was a therapist named Cary who taught me to drive a car with hand controls. These cars are equipped with a lever on the left side of the steering column for accelerating and braking, and a knob mounted on the steering wheel for one-hand steering. Learning to drive with hand controls is like learning to drive all over again. My reflexes had to be retrained so I would react with my hands instead of my feet. Anybody who would climb into the passenger seat with a quad learning to drive has to be a daredevil or some kind of nut. I don't know why Cary wanted to do it, but I'm glad he did.

Driving the van was a real chore at first even though all the controls were power-assisted. On my first day behind the wheel, my arms felt weak and I did not feel very confident. But Cary said go, so off I went. He directed me through the neighborhood around the hospital, and my first drive looked like something out of a Laurel and Hardy movie. It seemed like I was everywhere but on the road. I drove up on the sidewalk, I mowed down about three mailboxes, and I came close to sideswiping some parked cars. All the while Cary was riding shotgun with nerves of steel and words of encouragement.

On another occasion Cary suggested that we take a long drive out of the city, this time in a hand-controlled car instead of the van. I was thrilled at the chance to get out of the hospital, so away we went. We drove most of the way on a four-lane highway. Then Cary told me to turn onto a side road leading up into the mountains. As I started up the winding road I could feel the strength drain out of my right arm with every turn. I said, "Cary, my arm is really getting tired."

"No problem, you can do it, Randy," he replied confidently. "Just keep driving." So I gritted my teeth and kept driving.

In a few minutes I began feeling panicky. "Cary, my arm is wearing out. I can barely turn the wheel." But he ignored me. Finally we rounded a big turn and my arm literally gave out. "Cary, I can't turn anymore!" I yelled as the car headed toward the embankment.

"Randy, turn the wheel!" Cary commanded frantically.

"I can't turn!" I slammed on the brakes with my left hand, and the car skidded off the road and stopped with the front end resting on the edge of a cliff. After a few breathless seconds, our panic turned to hilarity. I put the car in park and we just sat there and laughed until we cried.

After I rested for awhile, Cary got the car on the road, put me back in the driver's seat, and said, "Hey, I've got a great idea."

"Go back to the hospital?" I suggested hopefully.

"No, we're not finished yet," he insisted. "Let's drive to downtown Denver."

"Cary, you're kidding aren't you?" I complained. "It's 5:00 P.M.—rush hour. You don't want me to drive in bumper-to-bumper traffic." But Cary wasn't kidding. So we drove down the mountain into Denver with my arms shaking from fatigue. *If the people around me only knew who was driving this car*, I thought, *they would scatter for cover*. Thanks to Cary's unflappable determination, I enjoy the great freedom of mobility in my van today, and that's a real blessing.

Another one of my heroes is Dr. Frank Kik, my pastor at Eastminster Presbyterian Church in Wichita. Frank came to our church in 1976 after serving as a pastor in Buffalo, New York, and as chaplain for the Buffalo Bills football team. Since we both had a great interest in sports, Frank and I struck up a warm friendship which has deepened through the years. His input to my life as a man of God and a friend has encouraged my faith to grow.

Frank visited me in Chattanooga shortly after the accident, and he also came out to Denver a couple of times during my rehab. He held my hand and cried with me on dark days, and we also enjoyed times of joking and laughing together. Whenever I acted like I was feeling sorry for myself, Frank chewed me out royally: "Don't lay around crying about your trouble; get up and get back in the game." Frank is often more like a tough-skinned coach than a mild-mannered minister. His straightforward approach has always brought out the best in me.

Finally, Bob and Lil Love, friends of our family for years, are my heroes. They've been like second parents to me. Since my injury they've gone to the wall for me. Bob has offered sound counsel regarding my ministry. They have backed me up financially when I needed it and offered me space in their corporate offices in Wichita. Their moral and material support has greatly aided the fulfilling of God's plan for my life.

Recently a survey was conducted among the students attending the nine high schools in Wichita. One question on the survey really interested me: "Who are your heroes?" I wasn't surprised at the responses our students gave. Most of the answers identified the rich and famous of our society—mainly popular musicians, movie stars, and star athletes—as the heroes of Wichita's teenagers. Their responses reminded me of my easy-living high school days and my preoccupation with sports. If I had been surveyed at that time I probably would have written down names like Joe Namath and John Havlicek.

As I struggled through the three toughest months of my life at Craig Hospital, I began to realize who my real heroes are. None of them are rich or famous by the world's standards. My heroes are the persons who selflessly open up their lives to me and try to make my world a better place. They aren't concerned about notoriety or gain for themselves, but instead they knock themselves out for me. I'm humbly grateful that God has blessed me with these people. They are the kind of people I most want to be like.

6

Peace in the Eye of the Hurricane

//

Early during my stay at Craig Hospital I noticed that most of the spinal cord patients were close to my age. Then I learned that the majority of spinal cord accidents happen to people between the ages of 19 and 25. This is the age group of risk-takers—bold, adventurous young men and women who often live as though they are immortal and take big chances with their physical bodies. Many of my fellow patients were victims of athletic injuries—football, snow skiing, boating, waterskiing, etc. Others broke their necks or backs in car or motorcycle accidents, some resulting from alcohol or drug abuse. It was sad to see so many young, vivacious individuals maimed for life as a result of careless accidents. It was especially sobering to look into the mirror every day and realize that I was one of them.

I was reminded every minute of the day that I had suffered great personal losses as a result of my injury. I had lost my ability to walk. Much of the dexterity in my hands and arms was gone. My injury had robbed me of the enjoyment of playing sports and forever complicated many normal, everyday activities. From the moment I woke up each morning until I transferred into bed at night, I was painfully aware of what I could no longer do.

In addition to the physical limitations which were so obvious to me, I became aware of a trio of negative emotions which threatened to cripple me from the inside. One of my greatest temptations at Craig was to allow these negative emotions—anger, fear, and depression—to sweep me away and rule my behavior. I was appalled at how many patients at Craig were not only the victims of the circumstances which caused their physical injuries, but also became the victims of the runaway negative emotions which accompanied them. I began to admit to myself that there was nothing I could do to change the fact that I was a quad. Short of a miracle, those losses were irreversible. But I decided to do something about the bad feelings which were trying to beat my insides into submission. Early in my rehabilitation I began to apply myself to master the negative emotions which threatened to master me. Wayne and I spent many hours battling our anger, fear, and depression by encouraging and praying for each other. When I felt defeated, Wayne moved in to bolster my courage, and I did the same for him. We became indispensable peer counselors and prayer partners for each other.

Like other victims of spinal cord injuries at Craig Hospital, I participated in reentry classes in between sessions of rigorous physical therapy. Reentry classes were geared to do for the patient's mind what the physical and occupational therapy did for the body. Hospital psychologists used the strategies of small-group discussion and role-play to prepare patients to reenter society in a positive frame of mind with their emotions under control. I benefited from the reentry classes largely because they complemented the support and encouragement I was already receiving from my family, my roommate, and other people God sent to minister to me. Many of the patients were so emotionally shaken by their disabilities that they required extensive psychological counseling to help them prepare to relate to the outside world.

After my first few weeks at Craig Hospital I had pretty well come to terms with my emotions. There were still times when I felt angry at God for allowing my accident to happen. But I began to understand that it's okay to be angry with God as long as I expressed my anger positively and productively. I realized that I could angrily shake my fist in God's face for the rest of my life demanding that He answer my "Why me?" question. But I had learned enough about the sovereignty of God to know that He didn't have to answer me. Instead, Wayne and I challenged each other to channel our anger into asking, "Where do we go from here?" We assured each other that, even though God may not respond to angry demands for "Why me?" explanations, He always answers prayers for guidance.

Some of my fellow patients were deeply mired in thoughts and feelings of anger. They were not about to forgive God or their circumstances for the hand of disability they had been dealt. Anger was so prevalent among the patients that I had a hard time convincing one of the hospital psychologists that I had my anger in perspective. One day she came into my room and sat down to try to "help" me. "Randy, I've noticed that you don't show much emotion. I know you must be harboring unexpressed anger inside. Do you want to talk about it?"

"Actually, Doc," I replied calmly, "I don't have any pockets of anger inside which I haven't dealt with. I'm not angry about my injury."

She looked like she didn't believe me. "Randy, it's okay for you to express your anger. It's important to let those deep feelings come to the surface. Why don't you tell me about it?"

"Because I don't have anything to tell," I answered, feeling a bit annoyed at her persistence. "Whenever I feel angry about my circumstances, I talk it over with my roommate and we pray about it. I don't have any anger buried inside to tell you about."

The more I assured her that I wasn't angry, the more she kept pressing me to vent the anger which she knew I had bottled up inside. By the end of her visit she got what she wanted. I was angry all right—angry at her for trying to convince me that I was angry when I wasn't!

Another negative emotion which stalked me during those first weeks of treatment was fear. Most of my fears centered on the unknowns of facing life as a quadriplegic. I was afraid of how people would treat me. I was afraid that I wouldn't be able to support myself or care for myself. I was afraid of being left alone. I was afraid of falling out of bed or out of my chair, drowning in the therapy pool, and a number of other real and imagined dangers which awaited me in the darkness ahead. I didn't yet know the scope of my limitations, and I was afraid I wouldn't reach my potential for recovery.

Wayne and I spent many tearful evenings together admitting our fears to each other one by one and praying through them. We discovered that if we ran away from our fears by burying them deep inside or avoiding them, they only grew larger and seemed more threatening. But if we talked about them openly and prayed about them, they began to diminish. We also learned that God doesn't sweep away all fear instantaneously. Each day seems to have its own new set of fears which need to be dealt with. Wayne and I reminded each other to use our fears—great or small—as reminders to run to God daily for His solutions. We tried to follow Paul's advice: "Don't worry about anything; instead, pray about everything; tell God your needs and don't forget to thank him for his answers" (Philippians 4:6, TLB).

There were also times when I battled with depression over my lost abilities, especially when I got back to Wichita. But I never experienced great dives of depression as some quads and paras do. A major reason for this victory was the ministry of Pastor Frank Kik in my life during my rehabilitation. Frank kept reminding me of Paul's simple but profound command: "Be joyful always; pray continually; give thanks in all circumstances, for this is God's will for you in Christ Jesus" (1 Thessalonians 5:16-18, NIV). It was hard at first to believe that thankfulness in a circumstance like my life-altering injury was God's will. But Paul couldn't have said it any more plainly. If I was to obey God's will in my circumstance, I had to start by being thankful. In his loving and straightforward way Frank kept prodding me to shift my focus from what I had lost to what I still had left—and to be thankful. I have learned that thankfulness is the lifesaving bridge over the crevasse of bitterness, anger, and depression into which so many people with problems fall.

In learning to counterbalance the downward pull of negative emotions by lifting thankfulness to God, I started with the basics: I was thankful to be alive. Often my prayers at Craig began, "Thank You, Lord, that You spared my life. Thank You that I didn't drown in that mudhole. Thank You for sustaining my life en route to the hospital and in those first critical 24 hours. Thank You for dissolving the blood clot in my lung which could have easily ended my life." In my prayers of thanks I realized that for some reason God had permitted my accident, but prevented my death. I filled my prayers with gratitude for His sovereignty in sparing me.

I was stunned to learn that the major cause of death among the victims of spinal cord injury is suicide. For many the shock of facing life without the use of their limbs is so great that they choose to end their own lives instead of making the most of their disability. I'm thankful that my Christian upbringing prepared me to meet and resist that temptation. Even in my lowest moments I never seriously considered suicide. Deep inside I knew that God was doing something. I didn't like what had happened to me, but I knew that God hadn't given up on me, so I wasn't about to give up on Him.

I'm also thankful that I still have full control of my mental faculties. My three-month stay among the brain-damaged patients at Craig Hospital was a sobering reminder that my accident could have left me with serious neurological problems. Most of the brain-damaged patients had suffered a significant loss of their ability to think or speak clearly. Don was one of the sad stories in the brain-damage ward at Craig. At the time of his accident Don was within six weeks of graduating from college with a degree in finance. He had already sewed up a terrific job in Dallas. But one night he got drunk at a party, fell out a window, and suffered serious brain damage. He was little more than a vegetable for a long time. Even though he regained a good measure of his mental function, Don will never fully recover from his unfortunate accident.

Mike was another guy from the brain-damage ward whom I befriended. Mike's level of thought and conversation was reduced to that of a young child. There is something refreshing about Mike's childlikeness, but it's also saddening to think that his mental development will never catch up to his physical size. For reasons beyond my understanding, God allowed me to survive my accident with my mind intact, and I give Him thanks for that.

I'm also grateful to God for a seemingly insignificant but providential incident which occurred about six months before my injury. My dad telephoned me one day and said, "Randy, there's an insurance agent in my office right now who is talking to me about disability insurance. I think you ought to come over and hear what he has to say."

The idea of signing up for disability insurance at that time in my life made me laugh. "Dad, I'm 24 years old and I'm in excellent physical condition," I argued. "Why in the world should I throw my money away on disability insurance?"

"It's something I hope and pray you will never need," Dad persisted. "But if something unforeseen should happen and you can't work, this policy guarantees you a monthly income while you're disabled. I think it's a good policy. Why don't you come over and talk to the man?"

I went over, partly to get my dad off my back and partly because I knew my dad wouldn't recommend something to me that he didn't feel was important. Disability insurance didn't make much sense to me, but if it made sense to him it was probably the sensible thing to do. So I took out a policy. Today part of my living expenses are covered by the monthly benefits I receive from that policy. I can honestly say that I would have preferred to pay the premiums on that policy all my life than to have cashed in on its benefits as soon as I did. But I am grateful that God made provision for my financial need even before I had that need. And I'm grateful for my dad's wisdom in the matter which prompted me to take out the policy.

I also thank God for my sense of humor. Under the dismal clouds of my injury and the ensuing tedious rehabilitation, it would have been easy to live out my days as a quadriplegic in the shadows of discouragement and disappointment. The temptation to look on the dark side of my experience never seems to wander far from me. But in the midst of the turmoil of frustrating, strength-sapping therapy at Craig, I began to see that God had provided a refreshing eye of joy and humor in the center of my life's hurricane. Some crazy events at Craig helped me discover the truth of Solomon's words: "A cheerful heart is good medicine" (Proverbs 17:22, NIV). I learned to laugh at myself and some of the funny situations I get into as a quad.

For example, one afternoon at Craig I got the wild idea to host an unauthorized field trip outdoors for some of the other patients. So I rounded up a bunch of my friends and we wheeled quietly down to the elevator. I headed them into the elevator car until they were wheel to wheel, then I barely got in myself before the door closed. Once inside, I discovered that we were all facing away from the door and that nobody—including me—could reach the buttons. So the elevator began going up and down and up and down at the command of those outside pushing the buttons. But every time the door opened, those waiting for a ride saw that the car was full, so they let the doors close before they realized that we were yelling for help. I was sure that the doctors and nurses were going to nail me good for this prank. I expected to be in a lot of trouble.

Finally somebody stopped the car and I was wheeled into the office to face a corps of angry staff members. As I tried to explain my good intentions, I couldn't keep from laughing because the whole event had turned out to be such a riot for me and my friends. Since no damage was done, I got off with a mild reprimand—even some of the staff members were chuckling about the incident too.

On another occasion my parents decided to take me, Wayne, and Patsy out to a nice restaurant for dinner one night. So we got all dressed up and drove out to a lovely place in Denver. We sat around the table enjoying a wonderful meal and a lively conversation; it felt so good to be out.

At that stage of rehabilitation my weak arms were still not under my complete control. In the middle of an animated conversation (like many people, I talk with my hands as well as my mouth), my right arm shot out erratically like it had a mind of its own. I was holding a fork in my hand at the time. As my arm flailed out of control, I inadvertently jabbed my fork into the backside of a woman who happened to be walking by our table. She jumped and yelped at the pain. I was so embarrassed I wanted to crawl under the table—and so did my family and friends! I stammered an explanation and apologized sheepishly. Luckily she understood my problem and graciously accepted my apology. Then she joined us in a good laugh over the incident. The ability to laugh about my foibles has been a lifesaver for me.

I'm also thankful for the incredible support I experienced from the people of my hometown, Wichita, Kansas.

During my first three weeks at Craig Hospital I received nearly 800 cards, letters, and gifts from the people in my community. During the rest of my three-month stay I averaged almost 15 pieces of mail a day. Mail call was almost embarrassing, but the feeling of support was indescribable.

The congregation at Eastminster Presbyterian Church, numbering about 1,000 members at the time of my accident, prayed for me, wrote to me, called me, and came to visit me. I have never experienced an outpouring of love like those people showed and continue to show me. They are an example to me of what a real church is all about: people committed to selflessly meeting the needs of others. The students and faculty of Wichita Collegiate School were also a great source of encouragement during my rehabilitation. Their prayers, cards, and phone calls helped keep me afloat through one of the most trying periods of my life. I don't know what I would have done without the incredible support of my community.

As I prepared to leave Craig Hospital and return home to Wichita, I was also thankful that I had a future. I had reluctantly accepted the reality that there were many things I could no longer do. But thanks to the encouragement and training by my heroes at Craig, there were many things I *could* do. Frank Kik had encouraged me to consider entering seminary to pursue a degree in counseling. Others suggested that I might become a minister. I also thought about returning to teaching and counseling young people, although I had some doubts that I could face them as a quadriplegic. I felt that I had lots of options. As I told a reporter from a Denver newspaper: "As far as I can see, the sky's the limit. Whatever I do, it will be something in which I can glorify the Lord. The Lord is great, and more than once I've said, 'Okay, Lord, do Your stuff.' He's always come through for me." I was thankful to face the future, confident that the Lord had me and my life in His hands.

Finally the morning came when both Wayne and I were to be dismissed from the hospital. We had avoided talking about our separation, not knowing if we would ever see each other again after being so close for three months. When we met in the parking lot just before he and his family left, we parked our chairs side by side and just held onto each other and cried. Soon my parents were crying; Wayne's wife, Patsy, and their two kids were crying; and the doctors, nurses, and therapists were crying. We must have been quite a sight, 20 people huddled around two guys in wheelchairs, all of us bawling like babies.

After a long and tearful farewell, Wayne and his family drove away, and I wheeled myself back upstairs to say good-bye to some other folks. I found my friend Mike lying in the therapy room being treated for a blood clot in his leg. I rolled up to his bed and said, "Mike, I'm getting ready to leave and I just came up to say good-bye. I know I'll probably never see you again, but I want you to know that I wish you the best and I hope everything works out for you." I don't know how much Mike understood, but he looked up at me from his bed and stuck out his hand to shake mine.

I said good-bye to a few others in the room and rolled out the door. When I turned around for one last look, Mike lifted his hand in a childish wave and said, "Bye-bye." Again I was choked with emotion as I realized the beauty of the friendships I had found during my rehab. I would have never known these wonderful people if it had not been for my injury. My friends at Craig were another evidence of God's love for me.

It was early November, 1981, and I had just completed three of the most grueling, faith-testing months of my life. What had begun as a simple obstacle course in the Tennessee mountains had mushroomed into a challenging daily obstacle course of transfers, physical limitations, and frustration. As I prepared to leave Craig

Hospital, I was grateful to have cleared some major hurdles in my rehabilitation. But the clouds of fear which hovered over me during my last few days in Denver warned me that some of my greatest obstacles were still ahead.

7

Safe Return to Home Port

//

After I was dismissed from Craig Hospital, Russ Meyer of the Cessna Corporation again provided my transportation on his private jet, this time from Denver to my home in Wichita. As the plane descended toward the Wichita airport, I stared out the window at the Kansas landscape which had changed into its drab gray-brown wardrobe in preparation for winter. *The terrain is not all that has changed since I left Wichita over four months ago*, I thought. I remembered how excited I had felt as I left Wichita for Woodfield Camp in late June. I was the picture of agility, strength, and health. I was independent and carefree. I had the world by the tail. Now I was returning home in a wheelchair. I was physically weak, vulnerable, and dependent on other people for practically everything. My feelings were mixed as the plane touched down and rolled toward the terminal. It felt good to be home, but I was uneasy about the challenge of fitting back into my hometown as a quadriplegic.

Dad and Mom picked me up at the airport, loaded me into the car, and headed into town. "We have a big surprise for you, Randy," they beamed as we drove home.

"A big surprise? What kind of surprise?" I prodded. The promise of a surprise revived my sagging spirits. Dad and Mom had been especially generous and supportive since my injury. I couldn't imagine what they had up their sleeves, but I knew it would be good.

"You'll just have to wait and see," they teased.

We turned into the driveway of their home and parked the car in front of their three-car garage. Dad helped me transfer into my wheelchair and rolled me to the side of the garage. Mom opened the side door and ushered me inside. I was flabbergasted! While I was in Denver my parents had remodeled their garage, transforming it into a cozy, cheerful three-room apartment for me. They glowed with pride as I rolled my wheelchair through my new home. It was fantastic. There was a bedroom, a bathroom, and a living room containing a small kitchen area and an exercise area. The doorways were extra wide to accommodate my wheelchair. Everything in the apartment, including a microwave oven, was designed to help me live as independently as possible. The apartment was a wonderful surprise, and I was deeply touched by another expression of my parents' love.

If everything about coming home could have been as easy as moving into my beautiful new apartment, my transition from Denver to Wichita would have been a snap—but it wasn't. As I neared the end of my rehab at Craig, I told everybody in the hospital that I couldn't wait to get home. The excitement I felt about completing my rehabilitation and returning to comfortable sur-roundings was genuine. But as I neared my departure date, I became aware of small, persistent pangs of rest-lessness and anxiety inside. My disquieting feelings seemed to be strongest when I thought about going home. *Why should I feel so bad about something so good as going home?* I wrestled with myself. *This is one of the best things to happen to me in four months.*

One day I admitted my strange hesitancy about going home to one of the counselors at Craig. "I'm ready to leave this hospital—who wouldn't be?" I began. "And there's no place like home. I'm looking forward to being back in Wichita. But there's something about this transi-tion that feels uncomfortable to me, even scary."

"What are you most looking forward to about being home?" he probed.

"We have a very close family, and my parents and sister have been with me all the way since my injury. We get along real well and enjoy doing things together. I guess the greatest thing for me about going home will be spending more time with my parents and sister."

"What about the other people at home?" the counselor pressed. "How do you feel about seeing your neighbors, your friends at church, and your students and faculty members at Collegiate?"

His question caught me off guard. I should feel fine about being with these people, of course. They had been writing to me and praying for me since my accident. They loved me. But a twinge of fear alerted me that I had a problem with my impending reunion at home with those who knew me before I became paralyzed. I had felt a similar twinge a few days earlier when my parents excitedly told me about the plans my neighbors were making for my homecoming. "They're going to tie yellow ribbons around the trees. Then they want to have a parade with you rolling right down the middle of the street as everybody cheers."

"I don't want that," I snapped. "No parade, no party, nothing. I just want to go home to peace and quiet." I'm sure my response was like cold water thrown on my parents' enthusiasm. The thought of a big, splashy welcome really turned me off. I didn't want a lot of hoopla, and I didn't want a crowd of people around me when I got home.

As I thought about my counselor's discomforting question in light of my less-than-unenthusiastic response to a neighborhood homecoming party, the answer suddenly seemed clear to me. "Because the folks at home have never seen me like this," I replied finally. "I've always been strong and active as an athlete and a coach. But I'm different now and I don't want them to see me like this. I'm afraid of how they will react to me and of how I will react to them."

I explained to my counselor that I was afraid of returning to the mainstream in my hometown as a quadriplegic. I didn't look out of place at Craig Hospital because everybody was in a wheelchair. But I was preparing to leave the safe, accepting environment of a world where paralysis was common to enter a world where a young man in a wheelchair would stick out like a sore thumb. It was a very uncomfortable feeling.

"Good, Randy," the counselor responded. "Your feelings are normal and you will learn to deal with them. Admitting your fear is the first step."

I appreciated my counselor's attempts at encouragement, but my transition back to Wichita was still tainted by self-pity and the fear of rejection. Inside I was the same Randy Storms, but outside I obviously couldn't do the same things I did before, and I was very self-conscious about it. So when my parents drove me home from the airport in early November, I made sure that nobody else knew I was in town. For over a week I tried to hide in the background where I felt unthreatened by the curious stares and questions which I anticipated from others.

I soon realized that my retreat from reality created a huge dilemma for me. By avoiding my neighbors and friends I was squeezing shut the lifeline of encouragement through which I had been sustained during my three months at Craig. My fear of people seeing me in my paralyzed condition was an obstacle I must overcome or it would grow into a wall which would block me away from those I loved and needed. If I was going to make it as a quad in my hometown, I knew I would have to respond with openness, appreciation, and love to those who had so faithfully loved me.

Furthermore, I knew the ball was in my court. I couldn't stand back waiting for my friends to warm up to me as a quadriplegic and sympathize with my fears. I had to take the initiative and adjust my attitude and behavior to accommodate their fears. The minority must always adapt to fit in with the majority; it doesn't work the other way. That's one of the problems with some disabled people today. They expect the mainstream to adjust to their disabilities and accommodate to their unique needs. Sure, society needs to recognize and try to meet the needs of the disabled as much as possible. Special parking spaces, ramps, restroom facilities, and other provisions are a great help; I'm all for them. But it's the disabled person's responsibility to blend in with the able-bodied world. We have to try to break down the barriers of fear which exist in many able-bodied people who think that disabled persons are weird or crazy. I learned very early after my return to Wichita that if I waited for society to accommodate itself to all my limitations, I would be waiting a long time. I had to aggressively move toward people and plug myself back into society.

Three wonderful experiences during my first month in Wichita helped expedite my healthy transition back into the community. The first was sparked by a phone call from my pastor at Eastminster Presbyterian Church, Dr. Frank Kik. "Randy, I just found out you've been home for a week already," he began. "Why didn't you call? Why weren't you in church on Sunday?"

"I just didn't get around to it, Frank," I answered weakly.

"You must come to church this Sunday, Randy," he insisted, obviously sensing my hesitancy. "I know it will be difficult for you, but if you don't come now it will be even more difficult later."

"I don't know, Frank," I balked uncomfortably. "It takes me so long to get ready in the morning. I don't think I'm ready to—"

"No excuses, Randy," Frank cut in sternly. "You get yourself up on Sunday morning and you be here." Then he hung up. Frank was right and I knew it, but I dreaded being seen by the congregation in my wheelchair.

On my second Sunday back in Wichita I attended Eastminster for the first time since my injury. Due to my time-consuming process of getting bathed and dressed, my parents and I arrived late for the service. When Dad wheeled me through the side door, Frank turned in the pulpit to greet me and a sea of heads swiveled curiously to follow his gaze in my direction. I felt like I was in a fishbowl with hundreds of eyes gawking at me. My face flushed hot with embarrassment as my fears about the reunion were realized.

Then something wonderful happened. Frank pointed to me with a grin of pleasure on his face. "I'm so happy that Randy Storms is home from Craig Hospital," he announced proudly, "and he's here with us today. Welcome home, Randy." Then the congregation exploded with exuberant, spontaneous applause which filled my eyes with tears. After the service I was greeted and hugged by wave after wave of my fellow church members. My fears about returning to Eastminster literally melted away in the warmth of their welcome. It was a very special occasion for me.

Dr. Kik was also responsible for the second event which facilitated my transition from Craig Hospital to home. While I was still in Denver, Frank told me that he wanted me to address the congregation at Eastminster when I got home. I cringed at the thought of being in front of such a large crowd. I was no public speaker. I was just the 25-year-old victim of a tragic, crippling accident. What did I have to say to all those people, most of whom were my seniors? When I returned to Wichita I secretly hoped that Frank had forgotten all about asking me to speak—but he hadn't.

During the week after my first Sunday back at church, Frank called me again. "You need to tell your story to the congregation, Randy. I want you to share what the Lord has done for you through your accident and your rehabilitation. You'll be speaking on Thanksgiving weekend in all three Sunday morning services. I'll be praying for you and I know God will use you to challenge our people." Before I could object, he hung up. As far as Frank was concerned, it was a done deal. I would speak to the congregation and there was no question about it.

I was terrified at the thought—not just speaking to hundreds of people, but being on display in my wheelchair in front of people who had seen me only as a virile, active sportsman. But I knew there was no way I could squirm out of it. My pastor had made up my mind for me.

The night before addressing the congregation, I stayed up late trying to figure out what I was going to say. I didn't have a clue. I showed up for the first service with my palms sweaty and my mouth as dry as cotton—and no prepared speech. The sanctuary was packed with people. Instead of addressing the congregation, I just began talking to them from my heart. I explained how my hasty decision to dive into the mudhole had transformed me from a strong, agile athlete to a quadriplegic. I thanked them for their love, support, and prayers which I felt during my rehabilitation in Denver. I told them about many of the struggles I encountered in adjusting to my new life-style. And I admitted to them that, without their prayers, I wouldn't be progressing as well as I was.

"The most important thing I've learned through all this," I concluded, "is that Jesus Christ must be the essence of our lives. He's the only one who can see us through life's difficulties. I can get by without the use of my legs and arms, but I can't survive without Christ. It took a tragic accident on Lookout Mountain to show me how insignificant everything else in life is compared to Jesus Christ. Sure, I'm sitting here paralyzed, but I have Christ in the center of my life. Some of you still have full use of your physical body, but you are paralyzed spiritually because you have not allowed Christ to take His rightful place at the center of your lives. So what if you have a perfect body? Nothing really matters if you're not at peace with God and with yourself. The bottom line in life is the condition of your heart."

The sanctuary was thoughtfully silent as I finished my talk. I sensed that God had taken the moment and spoken through my unplanned words. I truly believed what I said, but at that point my faith was more in my head than in my experience. I had a lot yet to learn about Christ's preeminence in my struggles.

The third highlight of my return to Wichita was an opportunity to address the faculty and students at my alma mater, Wichita Collegiate School, in early December. I hadn't seen most of the students since before my injury. I had the same misgivings about appearing before them in a wheelchair that I felt at Eastminster. As I rode to the school that day, I thought about the cards, letters, and gifts the students had sent to me while I was in Denver. I remembered with a smile the handmade birthday cards the Collegiate preschoolers and kindergartners had mailed to me on my twenty-fifth birthday. Despite my fears about the reunion, I knew I couldn't ignore or avoid the kids who had so warmly encouraged me during my stay at Craig. I had to face them and thank them.

"I woke up this morning with a lot of apprehension about being here today," I began as I looked across the student body. "I haven't been around Collegiate for over five months and I was a little nervous about how you would react to me. But you can't stay away from the people who mean the most to you, and you guys mean a lot to me. I can't express to you how much your cards, letters, gifts, and phone calls meant to me. You'll never know how special you make me feel. Thanks to you, it really is a pleasure being back home."

As the kids listened with wide-eyed interest, I described my accident and my struggle to understand God's purposes in my situation. I spoke to them about the importance of allowing Jesus Christ to be the center of their lives, and I challenged them not to allow their struggles to beat them. About halfway through my talk I noticed that many of the students were in tears. I was suddenly aware that these kids, who had invested themselves in me through their prayers and love, were just happy to see that I was okay. I was deeply moved by their openness and sensitivity to my talk.

After my talk a few kids bravely ventured forward to greet me. A wisp of caution seemed to tinge their smiles as they silently wondered, *Just how much has this accident changed Randy Storms?* But I welcomed each student from my wheelchair with a warm embrace and a sincere "How have you been?" Then we talked about the good times we had enjoyed together in the past. Soon there was a long line of kids filing by to offer their hugs and tearfully express their love. They crowded around me to share stories about their sports accomplishments and tell their corny jokes. I told them some of my funny stories from Craig Hospital and laughed with them about shrinking to my new height of four feet two inches in the wheelchair.

Shortly after my visit to Collegiate I learned that the students had dedicated the yearbook, *Collegian*, to me. I was deeply moved when I read the dedication page:

> Randy Storms is a smiling and shining example of the Collegiate principle, *Proba Te Dignum*— Latin for "prove yourself worthy." Randy's unshakable faith in dealing with a tragic accident is indeed an inspiring exemplar for all of us. . . . We of the Collegian staff wholeheartedly dedicate the 1982 yearbook to Randy, honoring his faithful spirit and fantastic vivification of our motto, *Proba Te Dignum*. We appreciate the way in which he has touched our lives and provided a challenge to each of us to reach high for our goals.

The tender reunion with my students was a special moment of acceptance and love that I will always cherish. The thought that God might one day direct me to spend my life ministering to kids in this way was the farthest thing from my mind. I had many other challenging obstacles to hurdle as I sought to return to a normal life. But it really felt great to be home.

8

Straining Against
the Current

//

After returning home it took several months for me to adjust to my new limitations in my old environment. Simple, everyday activities which only took me minutes to perform before my injury now consumed hours. More than half my morning was expended in just getting up, bathing, dressing, and preparing and eating breakfast. Then there were the daily exercises and trips to the aquatic center for physical therapy and swimming. Since I didn't yet have my own van, every trip in the car was a major operation requiring a family member or friend to help me transfer, stow my wheelchair, and drive me to and from my destination. By the end of the day I was worn out, and I still faced the tasks of undressing, brushing my teeth, and transferring into bed. Settling into daily life as a quadriplegic was a full-time job.

The day-to-day strain of adjusting to the routine in my new surroundings was offset by occasional telephone conversations with my friend from Craig, Wayne Hazel. Just as we had done during our three months together in the hospital, Wayne and I kept tabs on each other's progress and encouraged each other to hang in there. When I felt like nobody in Wichita understood my struggle, I called Wayne. He knew exactly what I was going through. Sometimes I was encouraged just by knowing that there was somebody in Kingston Springs, Tennessee, who understood the difficulties I faced.

Beginning in the middle of 1982 I devoted my full

energies to one of the most frustrating, character-building endeavors I have ever undertaken: learning how to walk with braces. Even before all the mud from Lookout Mountain had been cleaned out of my ears after my accident, before I fully understood the extent of my injury, my parents had taken a firm, faith-filled stand: Randy will walk again. Their contagious faith infected me, even though none of my doctors at Craig Hospital concurred with our hopeful prognosis. I confidently stated to a newspaper reporter before leaving Craig: "I truly believe I will walk again." I wasn't lost in a world of fantasy, superspiritual hype, or self-delusion. I believed in God, I believed in prayer, I believed in miracles, and I believed in myself. Neither I nor my parents made any rash predictions about when, where, or how, but we were confident that the Lord would get me back on my feet somehow. We prayed fervently that God would open the doors of a miracle for us and show us what we must do to walk through them. I did not pursue the purchase of a specially equipped van right away because I had high hopes that I wouldn't need it for long.

While I was busy with the daily grind of exercise, therapy, and learning to live on my own, Dad and Mom were scouring the country for the newest and best rehabilitation methods for spinal cord injury patients. They telephoned hospitals and clinics asking about walking therapy. They mailed away for countless brochures. Then in July 1982, one year after my accident, my parents and I discovered what we thought was God's answer to our prayers. We learned about a walking clinic in Des Plaines, Illinois, offering a new experimental program of physical therapy for the victims of spinal cord injury. We eagerly began to correspond with the clinic. Soon my parents sent in my application for treatment, and we were thrilled to receive confirmation that I had been accepted for treatment.

The program centered around a sophisticated electronic muscle-stimulation device called the Myo-Flex.

The promising reports we received described paras and quads on their feet and walking in body braces after Myo-Flex treatments. I had already acquired a body brace, so we loaded it in the car and drove to the Des Plaines clinic. Our hopes were sky-high.

The first phase of my walking therapy at the clinic required several sessions on the Myo-Flex, which kind of resembled a cross between an electrocardiograph and an automobile battery charger. I was instructed to lie on a table while several small pads were attached to my back, legs, arms, and hands. An electrical wire ran from each pad to the machine. Once I was wired up, the Myo-Flex sent a mild electrical current through my dormant muscles with a buzzing sensation which reminded me of a muscle vibrator. The Myo-Flex charge was designed to mimic brain-to-muscle stimulation—which was lost when I broke my neck—by bypassing the severed spinal cord. Therapists theorized that consistent electrical stimulation treatments would pave the way for muscles to be repatterned to walk. It was hoped that Myo-Flex-assisted patients would eventually be able to support their own weight and ambulate with the aid of braces, crutches, or walkers. As I lay quietly receiving my first Myo-Flex treatments, I prayed that they were right.

After several days of treatments I was ready to experiment with patterning in the body brace. On the day of my appointment I waited anxiously for my turn to come. I watched as other patients were strapped into their braces, positioned between the parallel bars, and helped to their feet and steadied by therapists and family members. I couldn't believe it. Quadriplegics like me were standing and taking a few halting steps. My pulse quickened in anticipation. I felt like I was on the verge of the miracle my family and I had talked about and prayed for.

Then it was my turn. The therapists helped me into the body brace, which consists of a huge corset strapped around the midsection, metal leg braces stretching the length of the inner and outer seams, and four padded straps securing the thighs and calves to the brace on each leg. Once I was cinched into the brace, the therapists and my parents gently lifted me to a standing position between the parallel bars. I was ecstatic. Tears flooded my eyes and I choked back sobs of joy. For the first time since my accident 13 months earlier, I was standing. True, the braces and one therapist supported my legs, and my arms on the parallel bars and a couple of other people supported my upper body. But that successful moment caused my faith to skyrocket. "I'm ready to go; I know I can do it!" I declared triumphantly after only a few moments on my feet. "I know I will walk again!"

We came back to Wichita with a Myo-Flex unit, and I settled into a daily routine of rigorous physical therapy which was tougher than any training I had endured in sports. In the morning I spent about 90 minutes lying on my bed hooked up to the Myo-Flex as the electrical current stimulated my dormant muscles. Then I was strapped into the body brace for about 45 minutes of patterning between parallel bars which were installed in my apartment. Each patterning session required three people to help me: two to support my upper body and one to pattern my legs by helping me move them in a walking motion. My helpers would slowly walk me from one end of the parallel bars to the other, turn me around, and walk me back. After 45 minutes of patterning back and forth, I was totally winded—and so were my helpers! Each afternoon I repeated the patterning exercises for another 45 minutes with a fresh group of volunteer helpers. In the evening I spent 90 minutes on the Myo-Flex before going to bed.

My helpers consisted of a wonderful group of about 40 men from my church who volunteered to work with me on a rotating schedule. Twice a day I had the rare privilege of fellowshipping with three fine Christian men who sacrificed their time to help me in the Myo-Flex experiment. With the help and encouragement of my family and my Christian brothers, I approached the tedious process of patterning with all the faith and never-give-up determination I could muster. I wasn't betting all my marbles on the Myo-Flex program. If the Lord wanted to use it to help me walk, fine; and if He didn't, fine. But I decided that the experiment wasn't going to fail on my account. I was determined to give it everything I had—and then some—and leave the result to God. I just hoped the result was the miracle my parents and I had hoped and prayed for.

I threw myself into the Myo-Flex regimen seven days a week like a boxer training for a championship fight. I was practically married to the machine and the body brace. Every morning and evening, either Dad, Mom, or Melissa wired me to the Myo-Flex and turned on the juice. And every morning and afternoon—day after day and week after week—three men showed up at my apartment to get me on my feet and walk me through my paces. Two men helped support my weight, one on each side, while the third helper lifted my knees forward to initiate steps—right, left, right, left. My job was mainly mental. With each mechanical step, my mind focused on coaching my legs to follow through with the artificial walking pattern. The goal was to train my Myo-Flex stimulated muscles to stand and walk without the benefit of feeling.

I worked the Myo-Flex program day after day and week after week. The routine was nothing short of plain hard work—drudgery. There were days when I had to force myself through every step of the patterning exercises. In my heart I wanted to do it and I knew I had to do it, but I sure didn't feel like doing it. If it hadn't been for the encouragement of my helpers—"You can do it, Randy"; "Keep trying"; "One more time, Randy"—I couldn't have kept up the pace.

As the weeks wore into months my strength and balance improved, so we moved the walking exercises from the parallel bars out to the driveway. Eventually I replaced the body brace with less cumbersome knee braces. But as hard as I tried to resist it, a sobering reality began to press in on me like a cold, dismal fog: My legs were not learning the pattern. More than a year of grueling therapy passed, but my legs were no closer to moving on their own than when I began the experiment. *It isn't working*, I began admitting to myself. *The doctors at Craig were right: I'll never walk again. I'm wearing out myself and my friends for nothing.*

I started writing some of my feelings in a journal during this trying time. Some pages were scribbled dark with frustration. Other entries were prayers for guidance and direction. Whatever I was feeling inside came out when I wrote. Often as I wrote, God reminded me of passages of Scripture which were especially relevant to my feelings at the time. I wrote them down too. It was as if the Lord were adding His words of encouragement in response to my expressions of frustration.

One morning after several months of patterning I wrote:

> I awakened late last night with thoughts of Myo-Flex. I was resentful, feeling like it's a waste of time. Every day I get stronger, but there's still no movement. Grant me courage to continue this therapy until December. Then make it clear in my mind what I should decide about the future. Show me over these next few months where You would have me be. Grant me peace and joy from above. Lord, Your will be done, not mine.
>
> "He gives strength to the weary and increases the power of the weak. Even youths grow tired and weary, and young men stumble and fall; but those who hope in the Lord will renew their strength. They will soar on wings

like eagles; they will run and not grow weary, they will walk and not faint" (Isaiah 40:29-31, NIV).

My friends and family members, sensing my discouragement and disappointment, rallied around me—especially my parents with their unflagging faith that I would walk again. Melissa was a constant source of encouragement during this time. But the frustration of the seemingly futile patterning exercises drove me to tears and pushed my perseverance to the breaking point. I experienced more anger and depression during this period than at any other time since my accident. I was trying so hard, praying so hard, and believing so hard, but nothing was happening.

One morning I wrote:

> I spent a restless, sleepless night last night. I talked and prayed to the Lord for a long time. I'm frustrated by the fruitless Myo-Flex therapy. I know I must give this experiment my best shot. But the frustration is almost unbearable, to the point of wondering if life is worth living. I feel like there is a noose around my neck being pulled tighter and tighter.
>
> But I have not given up. I must live one day at a time to be fruitful. Lord, please love me and accept me as I am. Let my heaviness draw me near to You. Grant me strength and wisdom. I feel trapped.

After nearly 20 months of persistent physical and mental struggle, I realized that I needed to make a decision about how long the Myo-Flex experiment would continue. In the spring of 1984 I committed myself to three months of extensive therapy at a rehabilitation center in Galveston, Texas. "This is it, Lord," I prayed. "I can't keep up this pace forever. I must get on with my life. If You don't show me some significant progress at Galveston, I will accept the fact that You have other plans for me."

I tried my hardest at Galveston, but things got worse instead of better. I suffered some complications during therapy which required corrective surgery on my foot, which terminated almost two years of daily patterning exercises. Though some of my loved ones urged me to resume Myo-Flex treatments after my recovery from surgery, I realized that the experiment was over. I never used the Myo-Flex machine or the braces again.

Even though my two-year effort was physically fruitless, I am able to look at it positively. I didn't feel defeated or rejected by God. Aside from occasional dips of discouragement, my attitude was good. I did the best I could for as long as I could, and it just didn't happen. I'm glad I tried and I'm satisfied that I didn't hold back. If the experiment had been a football game or a basketball game, the coach probably would have said, "It's too bad we lost the game, but you played your heart out, Randy. You gave 100 percent and I'm proud of you."

Even though the patterning project did not produce the gains I had hoped for, the experience produced other gains which I still enjoy and cherish today. Physically, the strenuous daily exercises helped me recover a significant amount of upper body strength and lower body tone. The two-year program developed my physical potential to its peak.

Socially, I gained many close friends among the dozens of people who worked tirelessly to get me on my feet. The experience of straining and sweating through a common struggle bonded us together. Some of my dearest friends today are from that group of men who so graciously and persistently gave of themselves to help me. My life is forever different because of the impact of these people over that two-year period.

Spiritually, I grew tremendously during the patterning experiment. The rigid discipline of my exercise program seemed to carry over to my spiritual disciplines. I spent many hours each week studying the Bible, Bible commentaries, and other good books. Since I was tied down for three hours each day by the Myo-Flex, I had plenty of time to read. I had lots of questions about what God was doing in my life, and I was hungry for answers. The answers didn't come overnight, but as I leaned into the Lord daily I learned to recognize His still, quiet voice giving me just enough to keep me going.

I worked hard to keep the communication channel wide open between God and me. I praised Him for whatever He was trying to accomplish in my life through the painful experience. Sometimes I shouted at Him with my teeth clenched out of frustration or anger. Sometimes I just offered Him groans and tears of discouragement. I know He heard me and sustained me through it all. Eventually I learned to seek God's will— whether it including walking or not. A couple of my journal entries read:

> Lord, I trust in You and I pray for renewed strength. I would love to walk again, Lord, but I want to serve You more.
>
> "And whatever you do, whether in word or deed, do it all in the name of the Lord Jesus, giving thanks to God the Father through him" (Colossians 3:17, NIV).
>
> May I grow in the knowledge of Christ. My main goal is not to walk, but to live a life devoted to Christ. May I be an imitator of Christ's life.
>
> Lord, grant me courage and boldness in dealing with others. Guide me, Lord, to where I can best serve You. Grant me a vision of my ministry.

My attempts to regain the ability to walk through physical therapy are not a denial of divine healing. From the day of my accident to the present, I have always believed that God could miraculously reverse my injury in an instant. I believe that God has the power to heal people. I also believe that God chooses to heal some people and not to heal others. I don't know why other people have been healed and I have not, but I don't have the right to question His reasoning or His judgment. He is the potter, I am the clay. As my Creator, He knows what's best for me. I know He will heal me when He sees fit.

There have been many times when my thoughts taunted me, *The reason God doesn't heal you is because you don't have enough faith. His hands are tied because your faith is weak.* I've heard that argument from other people too. When I was still in the hospital in Chattanooga, a minister we'd never met called my dad on the phone and boldly proclaimed, "All you have to do is believe, and Randy will be on his feet and out of there." If I really believed that God hasn't healed me because I don't have enough faith, I'd chuck the whole thing. Faith is an important part of healing, and I continue to exercise my faith in God's healing power. But my study of Scripture and my experience has taught me that there's more to healing than just believing it can happen. Believing is our part, and my parents and I believe God can raise me out of this wheelchair. But God has the bigger part, and far be it from me to explain why—or worse yet, to complain because He hasn't yet exercised His power to heal me.

Some people have boldly told me that since God hasn't healed me, I must have sin in my life. But if God can't heal anybody with sin in his life, He wouldn't have any candidates for healing—including me. I hope and pray that I'm growing in maturity; but I'm not perfect. Even the apostle Paul, the spiritual giant of the New

Testament, complained about a thorn in his flesh. We're not sure what his problem was, but he asked God to remove it three times and the answer was no. Paul's life was full of struggle and pain, yet his writings did not focus on how to escape life's hurts and troubles, but on how to glorify God in the midst of them.

I believe in healing, but I have a big problem with the "health-and-wealth" teaching which claims that God doesn't want anyone to be physically or materially impoverished. In my judgment that claim just doesn't stand up to the teaching of Scripture. The Bible repeatedly calls believers to lives of suffering. The apostle Paul spent virtually his entire Christian life in poverty and pain as a servant of Jesus Christ. That's what we are called to, though perhaps not to the degree that Paul suffered. I have no right to pray, "Lord, make me comfortable," but rather, "Lord, let Your will be done through my life and circumstances no matter what the cost is to me." My experience in the wheelchair is helping me understand that real health and wealth only come when I am committed to performing His will.

The call to suffer does not prevent me from seeking to escape my wheelchair by praying for a miraculous healing. At least once a week I specifically pray for God to heal my injury and allow me to walk again. I don't think it's wrong to pray for that. But I also pray, "Lord, may Your will be done in my life, and give me the grace to accept it." I've had people lay hands on me and pray for my healing according to the Scriptures. We're commanded to do it; it's right. But when I follow the scriptural formula the best I know how and the desired result doesn't happen, I have no grounds to be angry with God.

My experience brings me back to the sovereignty of God. Why does God choose to heal some and not others? It's not for me to know or to contest. It's enough for me to know that I'm His, that He has my best interests at heart, and that He's going to take care of me. Beyond that I can't worry about the fact that I do my running around on wheels instead of legs. I have to make the best of my situation until He changes it.

By the middle of 1984 my two-year walking experiment was over. My valiant attempt to learn how to walk through the latest advances in medical technology and physical therapy had failed, but I didn't give up hope in the Lord or in medical science. I know God can repair my severed spinal cord in an instant, and I continue to pray for that to happen. I'm confident that great advances in medical technology will eventually produce miraculous methods for treating spinal cord injuries. I sincerely believe that scientific breakthroughs will have many paras and quads on their feet in the first decade of the twenty-first century.

As I turned my attention from my body brace to the life ahead of me, I faced another large and clouded obstacle: *I didn't have a life ahead of me.* The first three years after my accident had been consumed with the task of recovering what I had lost in my collision with the mudhole. My aggressive, never-give-up approach to my rehabilitation had helped me reach the pinnacle of my physical potential, but I had no game plan for the rest of my life. The dreams of my life lay shattered on a Tennessee mountainside and the place inside me where those dreams had grown and thrived was empty.

9

Uncharted Waters Ahead

//

In July 1984, at the conclusion of the Myo-Flex walking experiment, Dad and I traveled to Los Angeles, California, to attend the Olympic Games. What an exciting experience! I was thrilled to sit in the Coliseum with 100,000 enthusiastic spectators watching the greatest athletes in the world "go for the gold." As a former sprinter, I felt the exhilaration Carl Lewis must have experienced winning gold medals in three sprint events and the long jump. As a former intermediate hurdler, I exulted in the excellence of Edwin Moses as he glided to a gold medal in the 400-meter hurdles. And as a runner who lost plenty of races, I groaned inside at the tragic fall which knocked American distance runner Mary Slaney out of competition for a medal. I could fully empathize with the athletes as they experienced "the thrill of victory and the agony of defeat."

As the Games drew to a close, I was surprised by another parallel between the athletes on the track and me—and it was a discomforting insight. Here were hundreds of young men and women whose primary focus in life for the previous four years had been to compete and to win in the Olympics. Their lives revolved around their training. They ate, slept, and breathed their events. For many, preparation for the Olympics had been a full-time job.

Now the Games were over. Each athlete had reached the goal of competing in the Olympics, and the cream of the crop had achieved the ultimate goal—a gold medal.

But now what will they do? I wondered. *Will they resume their educations, return to their jobs, begin preparing for the 1988 Games, or retire from athletics and launch into careers? The Games have been their dream for years, but the dream is over.* I could empathize with the athletes whose dreams had ended with the closing ceremonies. I hoped that each of them had a new dream to carry them on.

Similarly, the summer of 1984 found me at a vital crossroads in my life. My two-year dream to beat the heavy odds against walking again was over. The challenge of getting back on my feet had been my major goal. I had planned every day of my life around it for two years. Like most of the Olympians I saw in Los Angeles, I had competed well, but I didn't win the gold. The walking experiment had been a tough but rewarding experience in many ways, but the experiment had ended and I was still in a wheelchair. *So what do I do now? Where do I go from here?* I thought uncomfortably as Dad and I returned to Wichita. I began to realize that I was as unprepared for life beyond the Myo-Flex as an Olympic athlete with no dream beyond the Games.

I thought about Helen Keller, the courageous blind-and-deaf woman, who was once asked if there was anything worse than not being able to see. "Yes," she answered, "being able to see but having no vision." As I returned home from my exciting trip to Los Angeles, I experienced firsthand the painful truth of Helen Keller's insightful statement. During my two years of physical therapy I never gave up hope that the Lord could heal me or that my situation could improve. But as I neared the end of the experiment, I became a realist about accepting my limitations and pressing on with what I had left. *Unless Jesus does something miraculous for me, this is the way I'm going to be for the rest of my life,* I admitted to myself finally. *I'm painfully aware of what I can't do. But what in the world can I do?* I had absolutely no idea what I was going to do with the rest of my life, and it was terribly unsettling to me.

At that point I had no dream, no goal, and no vision of what I wanted to be, where I wanted to go, or what I wanted to do. But unlike most other people my age without a dream, my options had been drastically reduced. Not only had my coaching career vaporized in a split-second on Lookout Mountain, but so had most other careers requiring physical mobility and dexterity. I knew for sure that teaching was out. My self-image of the youthful, athletic, popular math teacher at Collegiate had been shattered by the stark reality of my disability. *Kids sought me out and crowded around me before my injury because I was a hero, but they will avoid me now,* I deduced. *They could relate to me as an athlete and a coach, but not as a cripple.*

Having quickly checked coaching and teaching off my list, I was completely out of ideas. I hadn't done anything else, I wasn't trained for anything else, and I wasn't interested in anything else. I was beginning to feel the desperation reflected in Proverbs 29:18: "Where there is no vision, the people perish" (KJV). I had come to terms with the finality of my injury, but I was dying inside for lack of a useful purpose for my life. Before my injury, I was cruising. My natural talent and easy success were whisking me through life with very little need for a plan. But as a wheelchair-bound former athlete I didn't know what I could do—I didn't even know what I wanted to do. Going from a life of easy choices to a life of no purpose was a real shock to my system.

I see a lot of people today wandering through life in that condition. They're struggling with their day-to-day existence because they don't have a dream for their lives. They're unfulfilled in their jobs, they're unhappy in their marriages, and they have nothing to live for beyond getting through another day. They have no vision and they are perishing.

As I thought about Solomon's statement in Proverbs 29:18, I imagined how it would sound stated positively:

"With a vision, people flourish." I recognized in those words a scriptural principle God wanted me to learn. People need a vision or a dream to be successful and fulfilled in life. This country was founded by men who had a vision for economic and religious freedom. They had a dream of finding a better life, and they worked to reach that goal. I think about Henry Ford, who developed the mass-production automobile when people said it couldn't be done. I think about the great inventors like Benjamin Franklin, Alexander Graham Bell, and Thomas Edison. Each of these men had a dream, a vision, a purpose which gave meaning to his daily existence and paved the way for his contributions to society. Successful people, both secular and religious, are people of vision. They see where they want to go, lock onto their targets, plot their courses, and go for it. People who dream great dreams accomplish great feats.

As I looked at my life after the Olympic Games, I began to see that vision is an integral part of being a Christian. Somewhere God had a plan for me, and His plan was the ultimate vision and dream for my life. After all, what better purpose could exist for me apart from doing what God designed me to do? *But if God has a plan for me, a vision for my life, where is it?* I pondered. *How do I find it?* In the first 27 years of my life God hadn't slammed me against a wall and forced me to accept His plan. Nor had He plopped His plan in my path hoping I would stumble over it. I began to believe that I needed to take some initiative if God's plan and I were to get together. I began to see God's plan for me as a valuable and special treasure which I must diligently search for, discover, and embrace. But I wasn't sure how to begin such a quest.

As I returned from the Olympics, I didn't know what I wanted to do, but I knew I had to do something. I was going stir-crazy in my apartment chained to the monotonous routine of getting up, exercising, eating, swimming, watching TV, and going to bed. I was desperate for some meaningful activity and I longed for a new dream in my life.

Once again, Wichita Collegiate School, and my father as headmaster, came to my rescue. Dad offered me the opportunity to return to the faculty on a part-time basis. Even though I seriously doubted that I could effectively relate to kids from a wheelchair, I jumped at the chance. My need for some activity in my life was greater than my apprehension about how the kids would react to me. Teaching really wasn't what I wanted to do, but it was something to do until I found my dream.

As I dressed for my first day back at Collegiate, I battled a nervous stomach and fidgety hands. *Will they ignore me? Will they make fun of me? Will they stare at me like I'm some kind of freak? Can I still teach effectively as a quad in a wheelchair?* The prickly questions continued to ricochet through my brain as I rolled my wheelchair into the crowded halls on the way to my first class.

Suddenly the barrage began. Kids and staff members swarmed around my chair reaching out to me for handshakes and hugs:

"Hi, Mr. Storms; welcome back!"

"Hey, Mr. Storms, I'm in your Christian Studies class third period."

"It's great to have you back on campus, Randy. We've missed you."

"I have a great joke to tell you, Mr. Storms. You'll love it."

My first day on campus turned out to be a wonderful antidote for my anxiety about returning to Collegiate. Yes, I got a few funny looks, and some kids were a little shy about talking to me for the first time. But I felt warmly welcomed, and my fears were quieted. I taught a couple of junior high classes each quarter that year and they turned out better than I hoped. But the new me really didn't feel very comfortable in the old role. Deep inside I knew God had something more for me to do, and it was up to me to seek Him for it.

During that first year back at Collegiate I began seriously seeking God about my future. The prayer for guidance became the center of my daily quiet time with God. I began to cry out to Him from the depths of my heart, "Lord, where do You want me to be? What do You want me to do? What is supposed to be the driving force in my life? I'm not just anybody, but I'm somebody. Who am I? I can't do everything, but I can do some things. What are those things?" Somewhere beyond my limited expectations God had a dream for me and I had to find it. But I had no clue as to what God's plan for me could be.

Like many Christians in our push-button society, I expected an answer from God right away—today, maybe tomorrow, a week at the outside. I prayed for a week and didn't get an answer. I prayed for another week, then two, then a month, but God's plan was nowhere in sight. I was tempted to believe that asking God for a vision for my life was like learning to walk with braces: I could invest two exhausting years or more without reaching my primary goal. "I'm seeking Your will the best I know how," I complained to God one day during prayer. "Why don't You tell me what I'm supposed to do?"

It was while wrestling with God in prayer that I began to realize that God answers prayer in one of three ways: yes, no, and wait. I already sensed God's no on a teaching career. But while I was beating furiously on His door for a yes on His plan, He was holding up the wait sign. I began to discover that a vision doesn't come overnight. Usually it comes through a lot of soul-searching, knocking on doors, seeking God's face, and days, weeks, months, or even years of time.

God reminded me that He had already prepared me for long-term seeking because my injury had taught me all about the discipline of waiting. As a quadriplegic, my entire life was reduced to slow motion. I couldn't do anything fast anymore—even if I wanted to. Through recovery and rehabilitation I had learned the discipline of working hard and waiting patiently for even the simplest motor skills to return. "Your prayer for guidance is like your rehabilitation," God seemed to say. "You must invest a lot of time and effort before you reach your goal."

So I continued to seek God's plan for my life through the '84-'85 school term. I prayed, I studied the Word, and I sought counsel from my parents, my pastor, and other Christians I respected. There were days when my faith soared and I joyfully anticipated what God had waiting for me. There were days of depression when I groaned from the pits, wondering if my prayers were just being recorded on some heavenly answering machine that God never listens to. There were days of bitterness and anger when I lashed out at God, "Do You know what You're doing? Do You have a dream for me, or are You just toying with me?"

Yet through those moments of angry questioning, searching, and wondering, I kept faithfully plodding after Him and seeking Him. I found that my pursuit of God and His dream for me was like athletics, rehabilitation, or any other worthwhile endeavor I had pursued. No matter how I felt, I had to keep going, I couldn't give up. It was easy to get angry or discouraged when God wasn't moving as fast as I liked, but I couldn't let my feelings interfere with my resolve. So I leveled with God about how I felt, but I keep seeking Him and His plan.

Meanwhile, day-to-day life went on. As I settled into a mode of seeking God's dream for my life, I also settled into a program of making the most of my situation as a quadriplegic. I moved out of the garage/apartment behind my parents' home in the fall of 1985 and bought a home of my own about six blocks away from them. As I started back to work, I decided that my day was too short and too busy to spend so much of it getting myself going in the morning. I can't just hop out of bed, shower, shave, dress, eat breakfast, and be out the door in half an hour. So I hired a young man named Chris to come in for a couple of hours every morning to help me bathe, dress, and accomplish a few basic household chores. Chris is a great guy—very capable, dependable, compassionate, and helpful. He's been with me since 1983.

Also, having come to terms with the fact that God was flashing me the wait sign on my ability to walk, I set out to solve my transportation problems. In the spring of 1984, I purchased a new Ford van which was equipped with a side-door lift platform and hand controls. I hadn't driven in three years and my Kansas driver's license had lapsed, so one of my first tasks was to renew my license at the Department of Motor Vehicles in Wichita. I felt almost paranoid the day Mom took me into the office. I hadn't practiced driving my van much and I was sure I would fail the driving test. I completed the written test and nervously wheeled my chair up to the counter to have it scored.

"You scored 100 percent, Mr. Storms. Congratulations," the clerk said.

"Thank you, ma'am," I replied respectfully, trying to hide my apprehension about the driving test.

She looked across the counter at me sitting in my wheelchair and asked, "Mr. Storms, do you have any physical limitations which would prevent you from driving a van?"

Are you blind, woman? I thought, concealing my surprise at her question. *Do you think I'm in this wheelchair for fun?* I decided that if she didn't see any potential problems, neither did I. "No, ma'am," I answered confidently, "I don't."

"Fine," she answered as she scribbled her signature on my form. "Here's your renewed license. Drive carefully." Then she handed my license across the counter and I left. I never did take the driving test.

Once I had my license I couldn't wait to get out on the road to practice. I had a few shaky moments getting my reflexes back, but I was soon barreling around town like a pro.

One of my funniest driving experiences—which I'm grateful didn't end up to be a tragedy—happened in Wichita. Like many similarly equipped vans, my van has no driver's seat. I roll up behind the steering wheel in my wheelchair and secure it in place with a clip on the engine housing. Late one night I drove a friend home, and as I got back into my van I neglected to clip my wheelchair into place. I slowly pulled out of the drive-way and stopped at a stop sign, preparing to turn. I checked for oncoming cars, then hit the accelerator. But as the van lurched forward, me and my unanchored wheelchair abruptly rolled backward toward the van's backseat. In panic I grabbed my chair's wheels and hurtled myself forward to hit the hand brake with my left hand. But instead of hitting the brake, I hit the accelerator. Again the van surged forward across the high-way and I rolled perilously backward. Before I could get back to the controls, the van dived off the highway and landed in the ditch at a 45-degree angle. The impact of the sudden stop threw me and my chair forward again and slammed me against the steering wheel and windshield.

When I came to my senses, I was slumped over the steering wheel and thought I must be bleeding to death. But miraculously, I wasn't hurt. I put the van in reverse and gunned the engine, but nothing happened because the rear wheels were airborne. *What am I going to do?* I thought frantically. *It's the middle of the night, I'm stuck in a ditch, and I can't get out to call for help!*

Suddenly a man's face appeared in the driver's door window and his eyes were as big as saucers. I rolled down the window and caught a strong blast of alcohol on his breath as he slurred, "Hi, buddy, how ya doin'?"

"I'm not doing too well," I answered, wondering how this drunk could possibly help me in his condition.

"Well, then, I better go call the cops for ya," he said confidently. He stumbled off into the darkness and, sure enough, in a few minutes four police cars were on the scene. The officers kindly blocked traffic and rocked the van until I finally got enough traction to back out of the ditch. I drove home thankful that I was still in one piece.

My van has been a source of independence; I can virtually go anywhere I need to go. Furthermore, the emphasis on access for the handicapped in our world today, such as special parking places, is a tremendous boon to my freedom. The only problem is that most of the handicapped parking spaces are too narrow for me to put my lift down, so I have to take up two spaces. Sometimes when I'm parked in a wheelchair space in a shopping center, I'll come out of the store to find another car parked too close to my van and I can't lower the lift. So there I sit waiting for someone else to finish shopping so I can go home. I still get a little impatient with thoughtlessness like that.

After many months of prayer I finally began to sense that I was moving in the direction that God wanted me to move. Every quarter I investigated a number of different job options, but I kept coming back to Collegiate. There was something about being at Collegiate that fit, but it wasn't teaching. I was beginning to believe that working with kids was a primary ingredient of the dream that God was unfolding. God seemed to be whispering that I could have an impact in the lives of teenagers, but at that time I still didn't feel that a guy in a wheelchair could relate well to kids. "Teenagers need somebody who's active, athletic, and charismatic," I objected to God, "somebody who can run with them and shoot hoops with them. They need someone more like them."

But the doors to youth ministry kept opening in front of me. In the spring of 1985 I was invited to speak at a Young Life all-city rally in Wichita and serve on the Young Life committee. I had worked with Young Life during my college days, leading a club at East High School. I greatly respected the ministry of Young Life and felt honored to be asked to serve on the committee. As a committee member I worked mainly with adults at local, state, and regional levels planning activities for kids. I felt safe in this role because my interaction with kids was minimal. God was subtly and gently moving me toward a ministry with kids at a speed I could handle.

In the fall of 1985 our Young Life program in Wichita was short of leaders for some of the high school clubs which were ready to kick off the school year. The committee approached me that September saying, "Randy, we don't have a qualified leader for the club at Southeast High School. You've had experience running clubs in the past. We need you to serve as a temporary leader to get this club rolling."

"I'd really rather not get involved at the club level," I resisted. But the facts were clear: If I didn't take the club at Southeast, it wouldn't happen. I reluctantly agreed to get the ball rolling in hopes that another leader would eventually take over. I've been the Young Life club leader at Southeast ever since.

Also during this time I had several opportunities to speak to other church groups, youth groups, and civic organizations, and I really enjoyed those opportunities. I gave my testimony and challenged people to look beyond their struggles to find what God had for them, and people responded well to what I said. Several interesting options seemed to be coming into focus and they all shared one common base: full-time ministry. But I didn't know if the Lord wanted me to develop a speaking ministry, a youth ministry, or something else.

In the fall of 1986 I returned to Collegiate to teach a class, work in the alumni office, and assist in fundraising for the school. I was convinced by then that working in the school was not a part of the vision, but it was something I could do to help my dad and the school as I continued to seek God's place for me. All during the fall I felt that God was bringing things to a head in my life and that I was approaching a decision about my life's work. Surprisingly, I enjoyed my ministry with Young Life in Wichita, even as a club leader. Several other little arrows in my heart kept pointing at teenagers, even though I wasn't seeing them clearly. Through all of this the Lord was bringing me through a gradual, deliberate 180-degree turn back to working with kids.

It really was a slow and difficult turn because I had been resisting it since my injury. Basically I ran from God whenever He approached the subject of working with kids full-time like I had been doing before the accident. In the same breath that I asked God to reveal His plan for me, I added, "And by the way, I don't want to work with kids anymore because I'm in a wheelchair and I can't relate to them." My time of seeking God's plan might have been shorter if I had learned the basic spiritual skills of surrender and obedience sooner.

It was through the slow seeking process that I came to understand better the sovereignty of God. I realized that God is always in control and that He has a plan, but His plan and our plans are not always the same. His ways are not our ways and His thoughts are not our thoughts. I had disqualified myself from ministry to youth because I was in a wheelchair, but God assured me that He doesn't disqualify anyone because of wheelchairs. He is the sovereign Lord. He can choose to use anyone, and He can use anyone He chooses. My job was to make myself available to Him and stop trying to disqualify myself.

If I tried to explain logically why I go to Southeast High School several times a week and hang out with kids, I couldn't do it. It's crazy to think that God can use some guy in a wheelchair to talk to kids. Yet that's the greatness of our sovereign God. He chooses to use people and circumstances that we would normally think He would never use to further His purposes.

Late in 1986 I knew God was bringing me to a point of decision concerning my dream. After more than two years of diligent praying, exploring, and counseling, two major elements of God's vision for my life had become clear to me. First, God wanted me to devote myself full-time to ministry, not teaching. Second, God wanted the focus of my ministry to be kids, not adults. And miraculously, God began to change my attitude about these two elements. Full-time ministry to kids was something I began to desire.

I knew that I had not been academically trained for ministry. My college degree was in business, not in theology, religion, Christian education, or counseling. Emotionally I still had reservations about my ability to relate to kids effectively from a wheelchair, even though every job I'd had was kid-oriented. But during my time of seeking, the sovereign Lord had cut through my thoughts and my feelings and spoken clearly to my heart. He had communicated to me, "Randy, I can use anyone I choose in ministry, even someone who hasn't been formally trained for ministry—and I choose you. And I can use anyone I choose to reach kids, even someone who doesn't think he can relate to kids—and I choose you. I can take what many—including you— consider a great tragedy and a great weakness and turn it into a great strength—and I will do so with you." God had touched my heart with a vision which exceeded my expectations, baffled my intellect, and numbed my emotions. It was God's vision for me, and I wanted it more than I feared my weaknesses.

I also learned through my seeking that God wants the best for us in spite of our weaknesses. For example, Moses was kind of a wimp. He didn't want to talk to Pharaoh, so his brother Aaron did the talking. Moses didn't want to get involved at all in Israel's deliverance from Egypt, but he was obedient and God used him. Jacob, the father of the 12 tribes of Israel, was a snake of a guy. He stole his brother's birthright outright, and yet God used him to found a nation. Jonah the prophet ran away from his calling, but God still used him to prompt a great revival in Nineveh. The Lord is so merciful not to give me what I deserve. I am imperfect and sinful, and I deserve death and destruction. But by His grace He makes all things—even my stubbornness and disobedience—work together for good.

As the 1986 Christmas season approached, I knew God had given me a dream, but it was more general than specific. God had clearly directed me to ministry with teenagers, but He hadn't said where, when, or how. God was calling me to take a gigantic step in my life. I knew the general direction, but I couldn't clearly see the next stepping-stone. So I kept clinging to the security blanket of my relationship with Collegiate and resisted any radical steps into the unknown. That security blanket was shortly to be ripped from my grasp. God was about to use another traumatic event in my family to force me to make one of the biggest decisions of my life.

10

Plotting a New Course

//

The story of Colonel Jim Travis and the battle at the Alamo has always been an inspiration to me. About 100 men were stranded with Colonel Travis at the Alamo awaiting attack by the huge Mexican army. The small band had to hold off the Mexicans in order to buy time for Sam Houston to rally the army of Texas. Travis knew that he and his men were hopelessly outnumbered and that everyone who stayed to fight would surely perish.

Travis called his men together inside the fort and said, "You all know that everyone who chooses to stay and fight with me will die. But we will go down in history as the men who sacrificed their lives so that Sam Houston and his army could win the independence of Texas." Then he drew his saber and scratched a line in front of him in the dust. "Those of you who choose to stand with me and fight, cross over this line." One by one they all stepped across the line. Shortly afterward the Mexican army swarmed into the Alamo and Travis' prediction came true. He and his brave band fought valiantly, but they were all killed.

In one sense the battle of the Alamo and the slaughter of Travis and his men was futile. But because of their commitment, Sam Houston's army had time to prepare for battle, and they defeated the Mexican army and won the independence of Texas. From the seemingly insignificant battle of 100 men against an army of thousands, one phrase has resounded down through history as the byword for commitment: "Remember the Alamo."

In the last days of 1986 I felt a little like one of Colonel Travis' men at the Alamo. God had scratched a line in the dirt in front of me and challenged me to make a commitment. I had prayed for a dream—a vision for what He wanted me to do with my life. Over a period of many months God had revealed the essence of His plan to me: full-time ministry to teenagers. His dream for me was a far cry from anything I would have dreamed for myself or what I thought myself possible of doing. He had done what I asked; now He was asking me to commit myself to live out that dream.

Of course, I was in no danger of losing my life as Travis' men did. But I was almost as fearful about the consequences of stepping over the line of commitment to God's dream. For one thing, I didn't know what I was going to do. The dream wasn't in clear focus. At that point I didn't know which area of ministry to kids God had in mind for me. In fact, I wasn't even sure of all the possibilities. Furthermore, I didn't know how I was going to do it. I was not a youth ministry expert or a biblical scholar. I was just a guy in a wheelchair whom God tapped on the shoulder saying, "I have chosen you to touch kids for My kingdom." But I was clueless about how to do it. I was reluctant to take any specific steps toward fulfilling God's dream for me because I didn't know which steps to take.

Up until December 1986 I felt no need to be hasty. I had a job at Collegiate and I felt comfortable there. I knew that working for my dad was only temporary, but it was such a positive environment that I was dragging my feet about leaving there to commit myself in faith to God's dream. In December 1986 another life-shattering experience for me and my family suddenly destroyed my comfort zone and unceremoniously shoved me across the line. Dad was dismissed.

Randall Storms, my dad, had been headmaster of Wichita Collegiate School since its founding in 1963. Dad wasn't perfect, and neither were the board members. They all made mistakes, but they always worked together to resolve their problems and forge ahead.

But in December the board suddenly turned on Dad. Ironically, he was relieved of his position by a newly-elected board of trustees, whom he was instrumental in appointing. This group of men he believed to be his friends and supporters, without warning, two weeks before Christmas, abruptly demanded that Dad resign, vacate his office before winter term began in January, and never set foot on the campus again. No thanks for devoted service, no farewell celebrations, just, "You're finished; get out and don't come back."

Our family was utterly humiliated and crushed by the board's brutal, unprofessional, and unethical action. Dad had given 23 years of his life to Wichita Collegiate School. Mom had taught in the choral department there for many years. Melissa and I had attended there. I played sports there, taught there, and coached there. The school had been a prominent thread in the fabric of our family. Suddenly a quarter-century of work, play, and happy memories crashed down around us. It was the saddest Christmas season we have ever experienced.

I am amazed at how Dad handled the situation. Nobody would have blamed him for being bitter, angry, and vindictive at the board for pushing him out so unprofessionally. I'm sure those kinds of feelings churned inside him, looking for a means of expression. I sure felt them. I wanted to blast the board members in no uncertain terms for their unthinkable cruelty to my dad. But Dad never said one harsh word to or about anyone. Instead he quietly accepted the board's action, explored other job opportunities, and accepted the position of headmaster in an independent school located in Augusta, Georgia. His positive response to this devastating turn of events has made a deep impression on me. I have always held immense respect for my dad, but I have never respected him more than during those dark days in December 1986.

Since Dad was dismissed, I was also out of a job. There was no way I was going to work for the board that fired him, so I submitted my resignation from Collegiate immediately. With one stroke of the pen I was suddenly out of a job. The security blanket shielding me from making a commitment to God's dream had dissolved before my eyes. God used the unfortunate events at Collegiate to draw a line in the dust and say, "Randy, now there's nothing holding you back. I challenge you to commit yourself to full-time ministry to kids." So by faith, mixed with generous portions of fear, I stepped across that line in January 1987.

For the Christian, commitment is a voluntary obligation which is essential to fulfilling God's dream in our lives. Once we have defined where God wants us to go, the next step is to commit ourselves to go there. The dream alone is not enough. We must consciously commit ourselves to it and to whatever is necessary to fulfill it.

My rehabilitation from a crippling spinal cord injury is a perfect illustration. After the accident, my goal was to recover as much physical ability as I could. In order to reach that goal I had to commit myself to whatever steps of rehabilitation were necessary to regain what I had lost. If I had not specifically committed myself to rehab, I would either be lying in a nursing home today or planted six feet under ground. Similarly, without a firm commitment to God's dream for my life, I would spend my life wishing and hoping for it instead of achieving it and enjoying it. The call to live God's dream is a call to obedient commitment to that dream.

The good news for Christians is that when the Lord gives us a vision He also instills in us the desire and the commitment to fulfill the vision. My love for the kids I work with has developed over the years until I almost can't contain it. I love to be around them, to talk to them, to laugh with them, to counsel them, and to cry with them. I didn't feel that way about kids before I began seeking God's vision for my life. My love for kids grew as I discovered His dream and stepped across the line by committing myself to it. The love I have for kids today is a gift from God in response to my commitment to fulfill His vision for me.

Once I committed myself to God's dream, I needed a strategy for reaching it. Commitment is an action, not an emotion. I knew that I couldn't just sit around *feeling* committed or the dream would never be realized. Commitment only paves the way for the step-by-step action which puts the dream into shoe leather. Jim Rayburn, the founder of Young Life, had a vision for ministry to teenagers. He used to say emphatically, "It's a sin to bore kids with the gospel of Jesus Christ." But he didn't just go around saying it—he committed himself to sharing the gospel with kids in ways which didn't bore them. Then he developed a strategy which put legs under his commitment. The rest, as they say, is history; the world-wide ministry of Young Life is the result. We must catch the vision for what God can do in our lives. Then we must commit ourselves to it, become excited about it, and strive to make that vision a reality.

During the first six months after I left Collegiate, God directed me into a period of personal introspection. I began seeking the Lord and outlining exactly what shape my ministry to kids would take. I thank God for Bill Nath, a wonderful Christian brother from my church, who met with me regularly throughout these months. Bill is a successful Christian businessman who is a strong example to me of what it means to serve Christ whole-heartedly in the workplace, the church, and the family. I first met Bill when he volunteered to help me with patterning therapy during the Myo-Flex experiment.

Bill used his skills and gifts as a planner and strategist to walk me carefully through the process of mapping out a game plan for my ministry. We prayed together, shared the Word together, and worked hard together identifying my gifts, setting goals for my ministry, and determining a strategy for reaching those goals.

It was through this process that I realized that young people have been the driving force throughout my adult life. Before my accident I spent a lot of time with kids as a coach, teacher, Young Life leader, and camp director. After my accident I couldn't get away from kids no matter how hard I tried. I didn't think I had anything to offer kids as a quadriplegic. I felt my days of teaching, counseling, and relating to kids were over. But God had a new dream for me, and teenagers were right in the middle of that dream.

Dick Gorham, former area director for Young Life, once told me, "It's amazing that you started out working with kids and then God brought you 180 degrees back to working with kids. It's pretty obvious that ministry to kids is what He wants you to do." It is amazing to me too. Sometimes when I think about what God has done, I just laugh out loud. Here's a guy in a wheelchair who hangs out with kids—and it works!

One of the avenues I explored during the months of strategizing was a staff position with Young Life. Several opportunities were presented to me at local, area, and regional levels. As I prayed about these possibilities, I did not feel free to commit myself to any of them. I cherish my relationship with Young Life and continue to serve the organization as a committee member and volunteer club leader. But the Lord seemed to say, "Randy, I have something else planned for you," so Bill and I kept praying and planning.

After several months of prayerful planning, my new dream had a name: *Randy Storms and Company*. Bill and I had hammered out a concise and pointed purpose which serves as my foundation today: *The ultimate goal of Randy Storms and Company is to share Jesus Christ with as many kids as possible.* I really believe today's young people are our nation's greatest natural resource. They are our future and our hope. If they don't develop a vision and a hope for the future which is based on Jesus Christ, this great country has nowhere to go but down. My central goal is to bring kids face-to-face with the reality and claims of Jesus Christ.

I was elated about establishing a goal, but Bill quickly brought me back to earth when he said, "We've only just begun, Randy. The goal is just a starting place. How will Randy Storms and Company reach that goal? Exactly how are you going to share the good news with kids?"

"I don't know, Bill," I answered, suddenly feeling a little lost in the process. "I've never formed a youth ministry before."

"Well, let's look at it this way," Bill pressed. "What have you done in the past which has helped reach the goal of sharing Christ with kids?"

"Outside of running a Young Life club, all I've done is tell my story and give my testimony at a few churches, conferences, and retreats."

"And how have those opportunities helped reach the goal?" Bill continued.

I thought about his penetrating question for a moment. "I'm no great preacher or teacher, Bill. But it seems that whenever I tell kids about how Christ has helped me overcome my struggles, kids are encouraged by what I say. They come to me by the dozens after my talks and tell me that my story helped them look beyond their struggles to see Christ at work in their lives. For some reason, from the first time I spoke at Eastminster and Collegiate, my unpolished message has made an impact on kids."

"That's where we start, then," Bill said enthusiastically. "God has obviously given you a story and a message of hope for kids. Until He shows us otherwise, I think your primary means for sharing Christ with as many kids as possible is to tell your story to as many kids as possible."

Bill's logic sounded right, but I still didn't see myself as a dynamic speaker. I was afraid I might commit the sin that Jim Rayburn talked about: boring kids with the gospel. But I couldn't escape the fact that God had blessed my speaking engagements in the past. So I took a deep breath and agreed with Bill that I should begin looking for opportunities to share Christ through a public-speaking ministry.

In order for me to speak to as many groups as possible, Bill and I decided that we had to tell as many churches as possible about the ministry. We hired a marketing firm in Wichita to help us produce an attractive, informative brochure. During the summer of 1987 we printed and mailed several hundred copies of the brochure to churches in Kansas, Colorado, Nebraska, and Oklahoma. In the fall I was excited to see a few doors open as a result of our mailing. I traveled to several churches around middle America sharing my story and a message of hope: There is a meaningful life beyond misery. To my amazement, my talks were warmly received and kids began opening up to the Lord and His dream for them.

About the same time we were mailing out the first brochures, I was surprised to find another large door of ministry swinging open to me. The Fellowship of Christian Athletes (FCA) is a unique organization dedicated to sharing Christ with high school and college-age youth through the medium of athletics. FCA reaches out to athletes through local "huddle" groups and regional, state, and national conferences featuring well-known Christian athletes as speakers. FCA played an important role in my development as a Christian during my days of college athletics.

In the fall of 1987 I was invited to speak at the Kansas state FCA conference. I was thrilled to look across an audience of hundreds of young men and women whose dreams, like mine at their age, centered on success in athletics. They listened intently as I described how my dreams were shattered on an obstacle course near Chattanooga, Tennessee, and how God had given me a new dream and a new vision for my life. A stream of kids came up after the meetings to tell me how my story had helped change their perspective on athletics and Christianity. I realized that these kids, who loved sports and competition as much as I did, constituted another target group for the speaking ministry to which God had called me.

In the middle of 1988 God opened yet another door of ministry for me: schools. Before Randy Storms and Company was born, several schools in and around Wichita had asked me to present inspirational, nonreligious talks based on my experience of growing through my tragic accident. As my church and FCA ministry began to gather steam, I realized the strategic opportunity of school assemblies and classrooms for telling my story. *Even if I can't say much about Christ*, I thought expectantly, *at least I can witness for Christ through my life and through informal, one-on-one contact after each meeting.*

I prepared a special brochure for school administrators announcing my desire to assist young people in finding their dreams, fulfilling their potential, and realizing that there is life beyond the struggles of school. The invitations began trickling in at first, and then they began to pour. My weekday calendar started filling up with school appointments, and I rejoiced at the new horizons for ministry God had opened to me.

Today, these three doors of opportunity are swinging open more widely than ever. I travel around the country speaking in church-related settings: services, youth groups, camps, and retreats. Ministry through the Fellowship of Christian Athletes occupies an increasing portion of my speaking calendar. I speak at FCA regional and state conferences, and occasionally participate in the national FCA convention. Recently I was appointed to the FCA advisory board for the state of Kansas. As a former competitor, I love to share my story with athletes and direct them to focus their dreams on Christ.

A recent speaking engagement at El Dorado High School in Kansas typifies the opportunities God has provided in the public schools. I spoke in a jam-packed auditorium and the kids seemed enthralled by my story of shattered dreams and a new vision. I identified with their struggles with school, parents, and peers and encouraged them that there is meaningful life beyond their pain.

At the end of my talk the student body blew me away with a spontaneous standing ovation. Afterwards scores of kids swarmed around me with hugs and words of thanks. I couldn't say much about the Lord during my talk. But as I talked informally to the kids who came to greet me, I encouraged them to trust their lives to the Lord and seek His dream for their future. I'm convinced that the potential for sharing Christ with kids on their campuses has barely been tapped.

As the outside speaking ministry of Randy Storms and Company grows, I continue my local ministry as a Young Life club leader at Southeast High School in Wichita. The Southeast club, which averages about 80 kids each week, has practically become part of my family. We meet together every Wednesday night for Bible study, crazy games and songs, and heart-to-heart discussions. I regularly meet with a group of club leaders to strategize ways to get more kids into club and reach them for Christ. A couple of times a year we get away for retreats, like the weekend ski trip to Colorado I recently took them on. As much as possible I schedule my outside speaking engagements so I can be back in Wichita for Young Life meetings and activities.

I consider the student body and staff of Southeast High School to be my primary mission field. When I am in town I spend several days a week rolling through the campus halls talking with kids from club, meeting their friends, visiting teachers and administrators, eating lunch in the cafeteria, and attending concerts and ball games. I realize that if I am going to share Christ with as many kids as possible, I need to be around as many kids as possible. The more time I spend among the kids, the more opportunities I have to relate to them, befriend them, and share Christ's love with them.

In maintaining a two-pronged ministry—home and away—I feel I enjoy the best of both worlds. As a "hit-and-run" traveling speaker in churches, schools, camps, and conferences, I am able to tell my story of shattered dreams and a new vision in a number of different settings. Kids listen to me because I'm advertised as a "popular speaker with an incredible story to tell." I don't get to know most of these kids in depth and they don't get to know me. I just tell my story and leave, trusting that it will impact their lives for months and years to come.

At Southeast I'm not a "special guest speaker." I live here, and they've already heard my "incredible story." I'm as common to them as the lockers lining the halls. This is where my faith must be lived out on a daily basis. These kids keep me honest. If I'm not walking the walk daily at Southeast, I have no business talking the talk in other schools and churches around the country.

Sometimes when the fatigue of traveling and trying to keep up with kids gets to me, I wonder, "Lord, is it really worth it? Am I making a difference in kids' lives, or am I just running myself ragged to keep them entertained?" It's in times like these when God's love intercepts me and reassures me that I'm in the mainstream of His dream for my life. Often God's grace comes to me in the form of simple notes like these, which I received recently:

Dear Randy,

I want to thank you for being my best friend. You're so open-minded and you really listen to me. You understand what I'm going through and you never put me down.

I can see your devotion to Jesus Christ and to bringing teens to Him. I wish every teen in America had a chance to know you. If so, in 10-15 years our country would be a better place.

Thanks for devoting your life to kids.

I love you.

Charlie

Dear Randy,

I think you have a true gift for communicating with us kids. You are the first person who has gotten through to me about the Lord. Now I have a relationship with Him which is real every day.

Thanks.

Kristie

Dear Randy,

Everything you have taught me has hit home in some way. I have dreams—ones *I* want to fulfill. But I also have friends who don't yet realize how important life with the Lord is. I know God's dream for me includes telling my friends about Him.

Thanks for sharing.

Ben

Today I am more at peace than ever before because I know I'm right where God wants me. That's not to say that God's plan for me won't change tomorrow or even this afternoon, but God has given me a dream. I am committed to living out that dream and I am content that God is working through me. Sure, there are days that are hard and hectic, days that are crazy with problems and conflicts. But I know this is where the Lord wants me; in spite of all the struggles, all the pain—this is it.

God's dream for me is so far beyond my imagination that I almost can't believe it. To think that I have the opportunity to speak to several thousand kids each year about Jesus Christ—it's beyond my wildest dreams. Who would have thought that God could turn such a tragedy like mine into such a triumph for Him? Certainly I didn't. But God is the God of the new dream and His dreams always have happy endings.

11
Holding Steady in the Daily Storms

//

If I had to select one passage of Scripture which has most helped keep me on track mentally, emotionally, and spiritually since my accident, it would be Romans 5:3-5: "We also rejoice in our sufferings, because we know that suffering produces perseverance; perseverance, character; and character, hope. And hope does not disappoint us" (NIV). I've not only read and studied this passage, I've experienced it. It was my life preserver when I was drowning in the pain and discouragement of my rehabilitation. It was my light at the end of the tunnel when I was lost in the dark hopelessness of my shattered dreams. It remains the rock-solid foundation which supports me in a ministry which I never dreamed I could do.

The good news of this passage is at the end: the promise of satisfying, fulfilling hope. If I needed anything after my head-on collision with the mudhole, I needed hope: the dream that something positive was on the horizon. Without hope I wouldn't have lived through my rehabilitation.

Before my injury, my hope was wrapped up in athletics and my physical abilities and accomplishments. I lived for the next game, the next championship tournament, and the coming season. My hopes were based on becoming a great athlete and a great coach. But in the weeks and months which followed July 3, 1981, I realized that my hope in myself was as shallow as the mudhole on Lookout Mountain. I had attached my hope to physical, material, and temporal values, and I discovered in a

.lit second that my hope was not the hope that "does not disappoint" which Paul wrote about in Romans 5:5. My athletic dreams were crushed that afternoon at the obstacle course, and I was destroyed with disappointment. Everything which kept me going was blown away. I've never felt hopelessness like I felt it in those first weeks after my neck was broken.

It was only after my injury that I began to realize that true hope is a spiritual quality which transcends the physical, material, and temporal values which had been my focus before. True hope is rooted in Christ's love for me and His plan for me in this life and in the life to come. It's a hope that isn't diminished in the slightest by the fact that I'm a quadriplegic. It's a hope that does not disappoint no matter what my circumstances may be.

As the truth of Romans 5:3-5 began to seep into my soul, I learned that this glorious hope for my life which does not disappoint is at the tail end of a spiritual domino effect which begins with suffering. According to Paul, the true hope I need for my life is produced by Christian character, which is produced through perseverance, which is produced through suffering. Before my accident I didn't know what suffering was. My greatest trials and tribulations came from enduring football and basketball drills, deciding which girl to date, and agonizing over what clothes to wear to school. My life was a trouble-free breeze. No wonder the hope in my life was so shallow and transitory. My experience with suffering, perseverance, and Christian character was strictly at the little league stage.

Then came my attempt to run the obstacle course at Woodfield Camp, followed by the physical and emotional traumas of recovery, paralysis, rehabilitation, returning to the mainstream, patterning, and finding a new dream for my life. In an instant I was transferred from the little league of suffering into the majors. Suddenly pain, struggles, trials, and tribulations like I had never known were a daily experience for me. In those first few months I couldn't see much beyond the first domino—the pain and struggle ahead of me in my life as a quadriplegic. I had no idea of the potential for Christian character and hope which my injury presented.

As I struggled to understand why God had allowed my accident, He challenged me through the people around me to meet my major league trials head-on with major league perseverance. My therapists at Craig kept saying, "You're doing a little better every day, Randy. Keep working, keep trying." My pastor and spiritual coach, Dr. Frank Kik, admonished, "Your injury isn't the end of the world, Randy. God has plans for you. You've got to hang in there. You've got to stay in the game." Encouragement to persevere kept coming at me from my family, fellow patients like Wayne Hazel, friends like Brian Linn, my students and coworkers, and from people I didn't even know. Whenever I tended to get soft instead of toughing out my trial, I had an army of loving people prodding me on.

To me, perseverance means staying with the program, remaining faithful right where God puts me. Like most people, I don't like trials and tribulations, especially those I face as a result of my injury. When I encounter pain or pressure, I want to find the nearest exit, I want to run from it. When I struggle with doubt over the direction for my life, I'm tempted to pull myself out of gear thinking, *I don't know where God wants me, so I'll just wait here and do nothing until He tells me what He has in mind.* I'm learning that perseverance means remaining actively obedient right where I am until God reveals His solution or His plan in His time.

The greatest challenge to the development of perseverance I faced was the Myo-Flex experiment. Every day for nearly two years I battled the temptation to give up on what seemed like a fruitless and hopeless attempt to gain the use of my paralyzed legs. I cried, I complained, I resisted. But thanks to the help and encouragement of my dear family and friends, I persevered.

On the surface, it may appear that my two-year ordeal *was* fruitless. For all that time and effort, I'm still in a wheelchair. But I came away from that experience far richer for having stuck it out when every physical evidence said to give it up. My spiritual life is richer today because I leaned so hard on the Lord for the strength to keep going. My relational life is richer as a result of the deep, meaningful interaction I enjoyed with the men who became my friends during my two-a-day patterning exercises. God is building qualities in my inner life today that I might never have seen if I hadn't listened to Him when He called me to persevere through the trials of my patterning.

My experience of learning to persevere since my accident has given me a new appreciation for the earthly ministry of Christ. I read the story of His life and death in the Gospels with new eyes. Ever since childhood I've understood why Jesus came to earth: to die for our sins and rise again to give us new life. But only since my injury have I been able to appreciate His perseverance to complete His earthly task in light of such opposition.

I think of the three years of His ministry—at first being adored and idolized by the fascinated crowd, then being hated, despised, ridiculed, and rejected. Yet He never opened His mouth to complain or ask, "Why, Father?" He persevered. I think of His brutal death and the ultimate rejection of the Father which caused Him to cry, "My God, my God, why have you forsaken me?" (Matthew 27:46, NIV). I'm amazed at Christ's perseverance to follow through with His mission in the face of total rejection. When I am discouraged, I challenge myself to believe that as long as I look to Jesus as the author and finisher of my faith according to Hebrews 12:1,2, I can also persevere through my insignificant trials.

A lot of the kids I minister to today have trouble with perseverance. Brent has a raunchy home situation which pushes his endurance to the limit. It's hard for him to hang in there, so he often gives in to the temptation to drown his troubles in a bottle. "You've got to hang in there, Brent," I counsel him. "Sure, you can go out and get drunk, and for awhile your problems are out of sight. But you're going to wake up tomorrow with a hangover and your problems will still be there. Instead of running to the bottle, you've got to run to Jesus. He's been to the outer limits of suffering and made it through. He can get you through too."

Some people have accused me of using my Christianity as a crutch because of my disability. As far as I'm concerned, my relationship to Christ is a stretcher. The Lord can carry me anywhere He wants. That's the great news I see in Philippians 4:13: "I can do everything through him who gives me strength" (NIV). There were days when I said about therapy or patterning, "I can't." But He whispered to me, "Yes, you can. I will strengthen you. Hang in there." Today there are days when I wake up thinking about the trials of daily life in a wheelchair. Sometimes I just want to roll over and say, "Lord, I'm going to postpone today until tomorrow." But I'm learning to say instead, "Lord, I would really rather escape this struggle than go through it. But You have shown me an example of perseverance, and You have promised to strengthen me. So I'll hang in there."

No, I don't find suffering and persevering to be much fun, but they are two of the dominoes I discover in Paul's spiritual chain leading to a quality I really need in my life: Christian character. I'm a long way from achieving the level of Christian character I desire. But thanks to the experience of suffering and perseverance I have gained from my injury, I'm also a long way from where I was before my accident.

As a physically talented, "together" young man, I looked at myself in the mirror and said, "Wow, what a eat guy! You're a successful athlete. You've got lots of friends. God is lucky to have you." I believed in Christ. I read the Bible, prayed, and attended church. I walked the straight and narrow—most of the time. I figured I was as good a Christian as the next guy.

But my traumatic accident made me realize that I'd never taken a long, hard look at myself beyond what I saw in the bathroom mirror. When I began to take inventory of my life from my hospital bed, I didn't like what I found. I saw a lot of junk in my life, a lot of ugly blemishes on my character: fear, doubt, selfishness, envy, and other dark characteristics which I had kept neatly hidden behind my image as the all-American Christian young man.

When I saw how inadequate I really was, when I saw that I wasn't the great, wonderful person I always imagined myself to be, it brought me to my knees. The foolhardy dive which had broken my body had also broken my spirit. For the first time in my life I began to pray, "Lord, forgive me for my pride. I'm not the person I thought I was. I'm not the person I want to be. And it's only through You that I can become what You want me to be." Persevering through the struggle of adjusting to life in a wheelchair is the principal way by which God has begun to answer my prayer.

I define Christian character as living out what you believe in all circumstances. Before my accident, it was pretty easy to live out my Christian values. I thanked God for blessing me with my athletic abilities. I prayed for strength and success as I competed, and I glibly told God that I would serve Him faithfully. I probably had Christian character at the time, but it was definitely kindergarten level.

Through my accident and the painful, trying events which followed, I heard God asking me, "Randy, do you really believe everything you've been taught? Will you still thank Me for blessing your life, even though your athletic abilities are gone? Will you still trust Me for strength and success in your struggles as a quadriplegic? Will you still serve Me faithfully even if you may never walk again?" It was only as I began to answer yes through my words and my actions that character began to mature in my life.

In addition to the physical trials related to my accident, my perseverance and character were tested through a serious, romantic relationship. In the fall of 1981, after I returned home from my three months at Craig Hospital, I began dating a girl named Kim. Kim was a fountain of encouragement to me during my two-year attempt to walk again. While my physical energy was being consumed by the difficult Myo-Flex experiment, my emotional energy and romantic interest were focused on Kim. Our close relationship caused me to start thinking about wedding bells.

But I had a major problem in my relationship with Kim's parents: They didn't like me, they didn't want to like me, and they refused to try to like me. First, I was a "born-again" Christian, and they didn't like their daughter running around with a "religious fanatic." Second, I was a political conservative and they were liberals. I stood for everything they disdained. Third, I was in a wheelchair. They treated me like a helpless cripple, an inferior specimen of manhood. They refused to accept me as a person or a friend, much less as a potential son-in-law. Kim was caught helplessly between her parents and me.

The pain of my traumatic relationship with my girlfriend's parents seemed to rival in intensity the pain of my physical trauma. "Lord, what can I do to please these people?" I pleaded in prayer one night as I lay in bed churning with anxiety. "My physical problem is bad enough. Why do I have to battle for approval from the parents of the woman I love? I've never felt rejection like this before. Why does it have to spring up in the most important relationship in my life?"

Kim's few attempts to bring me and her parents together socially ended up in heated confrontations. The bottom-line issue was my disability. No matter what we started talking about, we always ended up arguing over my suitability for their daughter. In our heated exchanges, Kim's parents said things they didn't really mean and, unfortunately, I didn't always help matters. Feelings of rejection prompted me to lash out at them in defensive anger. I said things I never should have said. My biting, self-righteous retorts felt good to me at the time, but they were not the right things to say. I only succeeded in pouring gasoline on the fire. The harder I tried to prove myself to them, the more defensive I felt and acted, further alienating myself from them.

Am I really as worthless as these people make me feel? I questioned myself as clouds of doubt darkened my generally positive self-image. _Will I ever be able to convince them that I'm a worthy partner for their daughter?_ I began to realize that perseverance had a much broader application in my life than just my physical trial. I was learning to hang tough in an area where I had never struggled before. As the months of our relationship grew into years, Kim and I prayed diligently about the seemingly hopeless rift which existed between me and her parents. Deep in my heart a dark, unspoken fear lurked. I was afraid that my inability to win Kim's parents was leading to an end to my relationship with her.

After nearly two years of dating Kim, the issue finally came to a head. Kim and her mother visited me at my apartment one day. Her mother came right to the point, "Randy, this relationship will never work. I want you to stop seeing Kim altogether."

"The relationship won't work because you won't let it work," I argued, feeling hurt and defensive.

But she refused to let up. The conversation quickly degenerated into a violent argument, and then into a screaming match. Kim's mother became livid and lost control. She grabbed me around the neck in a choke hold and had to be physically removed from my home. I was terribly shaken by the incident and deeply disturbed that I was powerless to prevent it or to solve it.

Kim and I dated after that incident for about a year, then I met privately with her. "This is one of the hardest things I've ever had to do," I began, choking back the tears, "but I must call an end to our relationship. Your parents haven't liked me from the beginning, and things are getting worse instead of better. Their rejection and antagonism is destroying our relationship. I don't see any possibility for change, and I can't go on under these conditions. I don't want to be the cause of problems between you and your parents. And I don't want to see us become enemies as a result of this conflict. I care very deeply for you, Kim, but I think it's best that we part as friends."

Kim tearfully agreed that we had done all we could to solve the problem. We wept in each other's arms for several minutes, then she said good-bye and walked out of my life. Our relationship ended in the fall of 1984, just before Christmas. For weeks I felt like my insides had been ripped out of me. I had lost a great friend. But despite the inner pain, I knew I had done the right thing.

As I think about my three-year ordeal with Kim's parents, I see how God built character in my life through the struggle. Ironically, the incident helped build my self-esteem. My relationship with Kim demonstrated to me that, even as a quadriplegic, I was still desirable and lovable to a woman, even to the point that she stayed involved with me against her parents' wishes. I realized that I still had the capacity to love someone romantically and possibly to marry someday. I also began to mature in an understanding of the Lord's timing in romantic relationships. Through my experience I recognized that the approval of the parents is essential in a potential marriage relationship for me. I acknowledged that marriage

.self is hard enough, and without the support of both *.ets* of parents it can be even more difficult.

As with my physical struggle, the emotional trial with Kim's parents forced my prayer life to deeper levels. "Lord, here I am again," I moaned night after night. "I can't handle this. I need forgiveness. I need help." Part of me wanted to fight her parents and salvage my relationship with Kim no matter how they felt about me. But as I prayed through those agonizing months, I found a growing part of me that wanted the Lord's input more than I wanted my own way. It was through persevering in prayer that God prepared me to make the tough, necessary decision to part with Kim.

After my relationship with Kim ended, I felt a great, painful void in my life. I needed some relationships to ease the hurt. I needed to get immersed in something positive. So I got involved in Young Life by working with a high school club. And miraculously, God lovingly filled my aching void with something which became even more valuable to me than what I had lost.

Getting involved with kids through Young Life came at an important time in my life. The kids didn't know it, but I was an emotional basket case. The Lord used the kids in Young Life to build me up after my devastating three-year war with Kim's parents. Their affirmation and acceptance helped me remind myself, *Randy, you're not the biggest jerk in the world that you have been accused of being. You're a likable, worthwhile guy.* Moving into Young Life helped me transfer my emotional energies from a hopeless situation to relationships where I found a positive purpose and a glowing future—relationships with kids.

Just as Paul discovered in his suffering, the experiences of suffering, perseverance, and character-building which have come to me through my injury have given me hope. I'm learning that all my struggles—no matter how unpleasant—will someday end. Every time I go through the cycle of Romans 5:3-5, I see God's handi-work at transforming hurt to hope. While I prayerfully persevere in my struggles, God faithfully works out His plan in me and in my circumstances. I've seen it work in my trials as a quad. I've seen it work in my relationship with Kim's parents. These experiences build my confidence and hope that God knows about my struggles and He will resolve them in His time.

I began to see why Paul audaciously claimed to rejoice in his sufferings. God promises to make good things out of bad situations if we hang in there long enough to let Him do it. As I learned to wait on Him, He transformed the misery of a split-second injury into a ministry which has eternal consequences. That's worth rejoicing about!

My ultimate hope, of course, is the knowledge that one day I shall be completely whole. If I am not healed in this lifetime, I will eventually meet Christ. Instead of rolling around heaven in a wheelchair, I will jump, run, dance, and maybe even play football and basketball again. I shall be more alive than I have ever been. The assurance of being whole in Christ's presence someday keeps me going.

One of my favorite hope-building stories is about a little boy who came home from Sunday school very excited one day. His father was reading the newspaper as the boy climbed up on his lap.

"Daddy, guess what we learned in Sunday school today?"

"Tell me, Son. What did you learn?"

"We learned that we could live like Jesus if we really try."

"Son, nobody can learn to live like Jesus. It's impossible."

"But, Daddy, that's what we learned."

"Son, it's impossible to live like Jesus."

"Daddy, could we try to live like Jesus for a year?"

"No, Son. We can't even do it for a year."

"Can we do it for a month?"

"No, we can't even live like Jesus for a month."

"For one week?"

"No."

"For one day?"

"No."

"For one minute?"

The boy's father was thoughtfully silent for a moment. "Well, maybe you're right, Son. Maybe we can learn to live like Jesus one minute at a time."

That's my goal as I persevere through the character-building struggles of my life: living like Jesus one minute at a time.

12
The Need for a Good Crew

///

While I was still in Denver, a friend of mine from Wichita named John came to Craig Hospital to visit me. After we talked for awhile, John said, "Let's go out for a nice dinner, Randy—my treat."

"Great, John! I'd love it," I answered, eager for any opportunity to get away from the hospital.

John wheeled me out to his car and helped me transfer into the passenger's seat. After loading my wheelchair into the trunk, he slid behind the wheel and we drove off toward Denver. "Where would you like to eat, Randy?"

"It doesn't matter to me, John, as long as the place has a ramp for my wheelchair." I suggested a few nice restaurants I knew about which could accommodate my wheelchair, and we headed for one that sounded good to both of us.

After a delicious meal and a wonderful conversation, John wheeled me over to the ramp and left me there while he went to pay the bill. He walked away thinking that my wheelchair brakes were set and that I was waiting for him to roll me down the ramp. I thought John had already paid the bill and that he was still behind me. So I rolled myself onto the ramp assuming that John was gripping the handles behind me.

As I began to gather speed down the ramp I suddenly realized that John didn't have me. I gasped and grabbed the armrests as my runaway wheelchair streaked down the ramp. "John!" I yelled helplessly as my chair hurtled toward the wooden doors at the base of the ramp. Behind

heard John cry out in panic, "Randy, look out!" I
ushed into the double doors with a terrible *thud*. The
doors swung open on impact and I tumbled out of my
chair and sprawled on the sidewalk at the feet of two
elderly women who were just walking into the restaurant. The humor of the moment got my funny bone and I
burst out laughing as soon as I hit the pavement. I
laughed so hard I couldn't even talk. I looked up at the
two ladies and their eyes and mouths were wide open in
terror. They probably thought I was stark, raving loony-
tunes, and I thought they were going to die of apoplexy
on the spot. But I couldn't stop laughing.

John came running down the ramp looking as white
as a sheet. When he saw that I was laughing he knew I
was all right, and he couldn't help chuckling himself as
the two elderly ladies scurried past us into the restaurant. "Randy, I'm sorry," he panted as he hoisted me into
my chair.

"No problem, John," I smiled. "I haven't had such a
good time in weeks." I couldn't keep from giggling as
John drove me back to the hospital.

Whenever I think about my tumble at the restaurant, I
remember one of the most humbling lessons I've learned
as a quadriplegic: I need people. It wasn't John's fault
that I crashed in a heap at the bottom of the restaurant's
ramp. I could have prevented it by paying closer attention. But if John or somebody else hadn't been there to
pick me up, I'd have been in big trouble. I get into many
situations like that which underscore my dependence on
people to help me do what I need to do—or *un*do something crazy I shouldn't have done.

For example, a few years ago some friends and I were
vacationing in my parents' summer home in North Carolina. One evening everybody else wanted to go out. I was
tired, so I opted to stay home alone and enjoy a few
hours of peace and quiet. I was tired of sitting in my
wheelchair, so I decided to transfer to one of the comfortable living room chairs. I rolled my wheelchair alongside

the other chair, locked my brakes, and lifted up the side panel of my wheelchair. With one hand on the wheelchair and the other hand on the living room chair, I started to transfer myself as I have done hundreds of times. I was right in the middle of the transfer when my wheelchair started sliding east on the slick hardwood floor and the other chair started sliding west. Suddenly I was suspended between the sliding chairs in an iron-cross formation. Then my arms gave out and I collapsed to the floor.

If somebody had been there, I would have asked for a lift into the chair. Instead, I scooted myself around the floor on my elbows trying to get the chairs together so I could pull myself up. The floor was so slippery that I couldn't corral either chair long enough to hoist myself into it. So I ended up lying on the floor for three hours until my friends arrived home to help me up. I was completely frustrated with myself for pulling such a stunt with nobody home to help me.

Before my accident I was totally independent. I was strong enough and agile enough to do whatever I wanted to do whenever I wanted to do it. As a result of my accident on the obstacle course, my physical abilities have been drastically reduced. Thanks to the rigors of rehabilitation and therapy, the muscles I still control are now strong again. I have adapted to my limitations and regained many occupational skills like dressing, grooming, and driving. Despite my progress, I still can't step up a six-inch curb or climb a flight of stairs. So if a home or store is not equipped with a ramp, I need somebody to pull me and my chair in and out of the place. I'm grateful for the handicapped access improvements which characterize our society, but I'm still aware of how dependent I am on people.

What I can and can't do physically is governed by the specific nature of my spinal cord injury. From the middle of my chest up I have clear feeling and movement like

...e else. From mid-chest down my feeling is unclear ...d incomplete—kind of numb or diffused—and I have ...o movement. I can tell I'm being touched on my lower body, but I can't distinguish hot from cold or dull from sharp. I can identify the general sensation of feeling, but I can't tell the specifics.

The feeling on the insides of my arms, closest to my body, is clear; the feeling on the outsides is numb. The nerves to my biceps are intact and I use those muscles. But the nerves to the triceps are severed, rendering my triceps useless.

The limitations of feeling and movement extend to my hands. From the inside of my middle finger to my thumb on each hand, the feeling is clear; from the outside of the middle finger to my pinky is numb. I can't move my fingers very well, but by combining the limited abilities in my arms and hands I have learned to do lots of things. I can drive, I can write, I can pick up objects of almost any size, and I can operate the telephone and kitchen appliances. Everyday life as a quad is a matter of making the best use of what I have and compensating for what I don't have.

Since my strength and ability is already limited, physical fitness is a high priority for me. I need to keep myself in top physical condition in order to maintain my active schedule. So I ride a stationary, computerized, motor-driven bicycle twice a week to stimulate the cardiovascular system in my dormant legs. I have a weight-lifting setup in my home so I can "pump iron" several times a week, keeping my biceps and forearms strong. During the summer I do plenty of swimming in my backyard pool. It's amazing how long it took me to build up my strength after my accident, and how quickly it dissipates when I don't work out. I'm stronger now and I can do more now than ever. But if I don't stay on top of my conditioning, I can easily lose what I have achieved. So keeping in shape is a daily discipline.

Even though I have learned to take care of myself pretty well, I can't do many things very quickly. Everyday life is a series of small inconveniences which I must deliberately and patiently overcome. That's where my need for people comes into sharp focus. My faithful aide, Chris, comes to my home every morning to help me with the time-consuming chores of getting up, getting bathed and dressed, and cleaning up the house. I can do some of those things by myself, but my domestic skills are so rusty that I don't even want to do them. I need Chris to help me free up my time and energy for more productive activities.

Similarly, when I travel on speaking engagements I have a corps of friends, like Vic Lawrence and Roscoe Yoder, who volunteer to travel with me to tend to my needs. I can get myself in and out of the van, and I can drive as well as anyone. But in order to maximize my ministry opportunities, I need people to help me do things faster and easier, especially when air travel is required. I'm thankful for the people God has placed in my life to meet this need.

At first, asking for help was very difficult for me—kind of a pride thing. I'd be straining to wheel myself up a ramp and somebody would offer to push me. "No thanks," I'd say confidently. "I can handle it." I wasn't used to being so dependent on others, so I overreacted to the side of "I-can-do-it-myself" independence. Sometimes I declined invitations to go out because I didn't want my friends to be stuck with the chores of loading/unloading me and my chair and pushing/pulling me everywhere. There were times I went without something I wanted because I refused to impose on someone to get it for me. I'm still learning to walk the fine line between dependence and independence in my relationships to others. Everything I've been taught challenges me to be as self-sufficient as possible, yet there are some things I cannot do well—or at all—unless I depend on others to help me do them.

...addition to my needs for people to open doors for ...e, accompany me during travel, and tend to countless needs in order to help me save time, I need people emotionally. On the outside, I may look different from most people, but on the inside, my emotional needs are the same as anyone else's. I need to be loved and appreciated for who I am. I desire relationships, friendships, and interaction with all kinds of people. I want to be accepted and respected as Randy Storms the person, not pitied, babied, or avoided as Randy Storms the quadriplegic.

My physical appearance is sometimes an obstacle for others who relate to me. The general public often doesn't know how to deal with paras and quads, so some people tend to ignore us, withdraw from us, or treat us as if we're foreigners or aliens. I understand this perspective because, for the first 23 years of my life, I pitied people in wheelchairs and turned away from them. I thought they were all mentally disabled as well as physically disabled. I shied away from close contact with them, thinking I might catch whatever they had and become like them. Needless to say, after my accident my perspective changed completely. I realize now that paras and quads are basically no different from other people apart from physical function. We do a lot more sitting down than other people, but our capacity to think and feel is the same.

I was shocked when, after my injury, I became the object of the misconceptions of others. For example, some people on the street automatically talk to me as if I'm an air brain, speaking in short sentences of one- and two-syllable words. Other people speak too loudly, thinking somehow that my ears are also paralyzed. Still others speak down to me as if my paralysis reverted my brain to childhood intelligence. Each misconception becomes a hurdle to normal, healthy relationships between me and those who don't understand my condition.

Perhaps the most common response I receive from others is the nonresponse of avoidance. In group social settings, some people refuse to talk to me because they don't know what to say. In public, many people walk right by me and pretend I'm not there. They don't acknowledge me because they think I'm some kind of weirdo that they can't relate to. They don't want to deal with the changes which may be necessary to get involved with me. For example, a stranger may not volunteer to push me up a ramp because to do so would change his schedule and make him a couple minutes late for an appointment. In some cases I believe people avoid involvement with me because my physical condition reminds them what could happen to them if they're not careful.

Sometimes I like to add a little excitement to the lives of those who pretend not to notice me. Once I was out shopping and came up to a curb I could not manage in my wheelchair. At that moment a couple of macho-looking guys strutted by me, acting real "cool." They were obviously showing off to impress any girls who may be watching, so they didn't pay me the slightest attention as they paraded by.

"Hey, you guys," I called to them loudly. They stopped in their tracks and turned around wide-eyed, looking like they had just been caught attempting to escape prison. "Come over here. I need you to do me a favor."

The biggest of the two guys walked meekly toward me, acting more like a scared little kid than the "cool dude" he was trying to be. "What do you want?" he asked apprehensively. He was probably afraid I was going to ask him to take me to the hospital for major surgery.

"Please get behind my chair and tip it back so my front wheels are up on the curb. Then roll the back wheels up. I'd appreciate it."

"Really? That's all there is to it?" he replied, sounding relieved. In a few seconds I was up on the sidewalk and he beamed with satisfaction. "Man, that was great," he

I thanked him for his help, and he and his friend
strutted away proudly. I've had a lot of fun turning
unsuspecting volunteers like "macho man" into experienced helpers of the handicapped.

It didn't take long after my accident for me to discover
that the sexual dimension of my emotional needs was
not diminished by my injury. Shortly after I arrived at
Craig Hospital, an incident in the therapy room demonstrated to me that my sexuality was intact. One day I was
lifting weights with some of the other men patients.
Suddenly the door opened and in walked a gorgeous
young woman, beautifully dressed and smartly groomed.
She was a vision of femininity, and our small group of
guys sighed deeply with appreciation.

I had never seen her before and I didn't know why she
was there, but I turned to my friends and whispered,
"Don't get your hopes up, guys. This woman has class.
She's here to see me." They snickered and told me I was
dreaming.

But as we watched, the woman spoke briefly to one of
the therapists near the door, and the therapist pointed
directly at me. My heart began to pound as the lovely
creature glided across the room in my direction. "Hello,
Randy," she sang sweetly. "My name is Julia. Would you
enjoy taking a drive in the country with me?"

My friends' mouths dropped in disbelief, and I was
astonished that my wishful prediction had come true. I
discovered that Julia was an old friend of the director of
Woodfield Camp. She was visiting Denver on business
and decided to pay me a friendly visit. We enjoyed a
wonderful afternoon drive together. I returned to the
hospital feeling grateful that I hadn't lost my appreciation for the opposite sex. But I quietly began to wonder
how dating, marriage, and sex would fit into my new
life-style.

Early in my rehabilitation I began to understand that

my masculine needs and drives were not paralyzed as a result of my accident. Attractive women still catch my eye and stir within me desires for intimacy with the woman of God's choosing. And, unfortunately, like every red-blooded male, I'm still susceptible to impure thoughts which I must prayerfully keep in check.

My three-year involvement with Kim, though it ended in disappointment at the time, confirmed to me that my natural desire for closeness with a woman could be fulfilled in a romantic relationship. If her parents had been friendly toward me instead of antagonistic, perhaps Kim and I would have married. But in His wisdom and timing, the Lord allowed that relationship to end. He helped me redirect my emotional energies into the rewarding ministry to kids which became Randy Storms and Company. I continue to date as my schedule allows, and I think I would like to marry someday. But my experience with Kim taught me that both the couple *and* the in-laws must be in agreement for a marriage to succeed. A positive relationship with my prospective wife's parents is essential to me.

As I settled into my life as a quad, I was very aware that I had physical and emotional needs which I could not meet without help from others. But the people around me were not mind readers, and sometimes they didn't notice when I needed their help. I began to realize that a communication gap existed between my needs and the people God had placed around me to help me. It was a gap I had to bridge by allowing others to understand my needs. I call that bridge vulnerability. I'm learning that I must be open to people, express my weaknesses, and humbly ask for what I need. Vulnerability also requires that I reach out to people who are uncomfortable around me, communicate with them, let them see that I'm perfectly normal inside, and put them at ease. I'm finding that as I remain open and approachable to others, I have

...e help and interaction I need. Ironically, my open-
..ss to receive from people also encourages others to be
vulnerable and find their needs met. The bridge of vulnerability is definitely a two-way span.

I'm also learning by experience that being vulnerable
sometimes hurts. I've opened up to people and been
dumped on and hurt. I've asked people for help and
been refused or ignored. I've attempted to initiate relationships, and the people treated me as if I didn't exist.
These painful experiences make me think of Christ, who
"disabled" Himself by becoming human. In His human-
ity, Christ reached out to tell us about God in terms we
could understand, becoming vulnerable to His creation.
His vulnerability resulted in rejection, pain, and death,
yet His unguarded love was the vehicle by which our
deepest needs were met. Christ's example encourages
me to keep reaching out to people in spite of the pain
which vulnerability sometimes brings.

Today I spend much more of my time in the mainstream than I do around other people in wheelchairs. I'm
uncomfortable around many paras and quads who use
their disability as an excuse to retreat from the world.
They're not vulnerable to others who can help them;
they're closed. They don't take the initiative to help
others feel at ease around them; they withdraw. They're
not straining to reach their full potential; they're just
coping. Unfortunately, people like this tend to perpetu-
ate the hurtful misconceptions many others hold of the
disabled.

I'm learning that, as I open myself to participate as
fully as possible in the mainstream, I gain credibility.
Kids and adults feel like they can talk to me about my
injury and the obstacles I have faced. My attempts at
vulnerability have presented great opportunities to tell
people what has happened to me, what I am learning,
and how I am growing. As I tell about my struggles, I'm
amazed at how my experiences help other people who

are struggling and hurting with physical, emotional, or spiritual limitations. I'm convinced that there is a lot of truth in the words to the song which state that people who need people are the luckiest people in the world.

13

A Rainbow Above the Clouds

//

After my roommate Wayne Hazel and I were dismissed from Craig Hospital in November 1981, we returned to our separate homes and immersed ourselves in the mainstream of life. We didn't live close enough to visit, but I talked to Wayne frequently by phone during the first couple of years. As the months rolled by we communicated less and less, but a bond of brotherhood lashed us together. We were like war buddies who had been to the front lines together. We had battled discouragement, anger, fear, and depression together during our rehabilitation. We saved each other's lives at Craig. Nobody understood my pain and struggle like Wayne Hazel.

After nearly five years apart, Wayne and I enjoyed a brief reunion in the summer of 1986. I stopped by his home outside Nashville for a visit on my way to my parents' summer home in North Carolina. Three months later Wayne, Patsy, and their children came to Wichita and stayed with me and my family for a week. We had a great time swapping stories and catching up on our respective lives. Wayne and I had taken separate paths. I was very busy—deeply involved in my church, Young Life, activities at Collegiate, and a busy social life. But Wayne had chosen a quieter life-style which reflected the comfortable pace of the Tennessee countryside. We enjoyed our visit and planned to meet again when our schedules allowed it.

 out a year later I called Wayne to set up our next
union. "How about coming to Wichita after the holidays?" I suggested.

"Sometime in January would be good for us," Wayne answered.

"Sounds great. Let's plan on it." Then we agreed on a tentative date. "I'm looking forward to seeing you again, Wayne. Have a great Christmas."

"You too, Randy. See you in January."

So much had happened since Wayne's last visit. Randy Storms and Company had been formed and was beginning to grow. Dad had survived his traumatic dismissal from Collegiate, and he and Mom had moved out of state. As Christmas 1987 approached, I grew excited for the Hazels' January visit. I couldn't wait to tell Wayne about the good things God had done for us since we had last been together.

Early in January 1988 I received a phone call from Patsy Hazel. "Randy, we won't be able to visit you as we planned," she began. She was weeping. A sobering fear hit me in the pit of my stomach. It was the same sickening jab I felt 15 years earlier when my dad called me in Michigan to announce that my friend Jack Chesky was dead. I dreaded Patsy's next words. "Wayne passed away yesterday from pneumonia. It happened very fast, Randy. It took us all by surprise. There was nothing we could do." Fighting through tears of my own, I consoled Patsy the best I could. But the reality of Wayne's death stung me deeply.

As I hung up the phone, my mind was clouded with questions which were all-too-familiar. "When, Lord? When does the pain and struggle end? Haven't I and my family suffered enough—even more than our share? Losing Jack Chesky was heartbreaking. Then came my accident, the trials of rehabilitation and patterning, the agony of my relationship with Kim and her parents, and the frantic search to find my place in the world as a quadriplegic. Dad's shocking dismissal from Collegiate rocked our family to the core. Every day I cope with the limitations of paralysis and life in this wheelchair. Now my soul-mate, Wayne Hazel, is gone. What could possibly be next? Will it ever end?"

I had been through the question-and-answer cycle with God many times before, and the answers always came back the same. With each new test God seemed to say, "Life is full of hardships, Randy, and all My children are subject to them. Many of the hardships are only minor inconveniences, but some are major, painful problems. That's the nature of human existence tainted by sin and imperfection. I won't remove all your pain and trials, because when you cease to struggle you cease to grow. But I do promise to go with you through your struggles and help you make the best of them. And eventually you will understand."

The seemingly endless stream of life's struggles makes me think about Paul's words in 1 Corinthians 13:12: "Now we see but a poor reflection; then we shall see face to face. Now I know in part; then I shall know fully even as I am fully known" (NIV). Each time the Lord and I discuss my trials, I realize that I am stuck in the "now" part of that verse. My understanding is cloudy and incomplete at best. I'm grateful for God's presence with me through the struggles of my life. But I yearn for the day "then" when I will ask, "Lord, what was it all about?" and He will finally give me a full answer.

In the meantime, God has given me a dream for my life, an ever-expanding ministry of reaching kids for Christ and helping them cope with their struggles. The core of my ministry is the Young Life club at Southeast High School in Wichita. I continue to serve on the Young Life committee, and I lead a club meeting every Wednesday night attended by about 80 kids. I'm on campus several more hours a week eating lunch with kids and attending football and basketball games. When I'm home

...ephone is a 24-hour hot line to the kids at South-
... I'm used to getting calls at all hours of the day and
...night from kids who just need somebody to talk to.

Recently I was able to help one of my kids at Southeast through a painful struggle in his life. I knew for several weeks that Tony had a drinking problem. He sometimes came to school and to club drunk. I tried several times to talk to him about his problem, but he kept putting me off. "I can handle it, Randy; don't worry about me."

One night Tony called me. "I'm in trouble, Randy," he said slowly, his voice filled with inner pain. "I guess I can't handle my problem like I thought I could. My folks are freaked out and I don't know what to do."

Since Tony's parents speak no English, I volunteered to contact an alcohol abuse center and arrange for Tony's treatment. I even picked him up and took him to the center to check in for his 30-day stay. I keep tabs on Tony's progress, and I know God will use this trial in his life to bring him close to Christ.

The circle of my ministry to kids outside Young Life continues to enlarge. I spend many weekends speaking at churches, youth meetings, retreats, and conferences. During the week I log hundreds of miles on my van driving to schools in and around Kansas to give motivational talks. Everywhere I go I challenge kids to catch a vision for their lives and never give up. When I step back and look at what is happening through Randy Storms and Company, I sometimes shake my head in wonder. Here I am, a frustrated athlete, rolling my wheelchair all over God's creation telling kids about Christ—and loving it. Who could write a script like this? Certainly not me. I'm amazed at the Lord's creativity and sense of humor in the task He has given me to do.

But even living out God's dream for my life has not been without its occasional nightmares. I'm aware every day that Satan is dead set against my growth and success in ministry. He keeps tossing roadblocks in my path to slow me down. His tricky, tempting suggestions are like the curbs and stairways which occasionally block my progress in the wheelchair.

When things are going especially well, I'm tempted by pride. *Hey, we had 100 kids in club tonight; I must be pretty sharp,* I sometimes think. Then God reminds me of my weaknesses and asks, "Who allowed you to have 100 kids in club? Who helped you do what you did to make it happen?" I have to pray every night, "Father, forgive me for focusing on myself today, for thinking too highly of myself. You are the foundation of my ministry and the reason for any success I enjoy."

Sometimes I'm overcome with feelings of insecurity and inadequacy, especially at the beginning of the school year when I face a new group of kids in club. I'm tempted to imagine how the new kids talk behind my back:

"Who is this guy?"

"I don't know, just some broken-down guy in a wheelchair who can't hold down a real job."

"He's old enough to be my dad."

"Why is he always hanging around with us? Doesn't he have any friends his own age?"

Satan also tries to disrupt my devotion with questions and thoughts of doubt: "You don't need to prepare for club tonight, Randy. Just let your personality take over"; "Why are you doing so much for these kids? They don't care about you or anything you do for them"; "You don't need to go to the football game tonight, Randy. You've been to several games already this year. Stay home and relax."

Disappointment is another big roadblock. For example, when our attendance on Wednesday nights slips, I get discouraged and wonder what I did wrong. Sometimes I spend hours helping a kid work through his struggles. Just when I think he's coming around, he stabs me in the heart with a thoughtless word or deed. Some kids drop out of Young Life club for no apparent reason. I see them

campus and have good rapport with them at the
n table, but they are slowly squeezing God out of
.eir lives and it makes me die inside. I go home crying,
and Satan uses the opportunity to sneer at me, "You are
a failure. Your ministry is a zero. Give it up."

Sometimes I get tired and Satan uses my weariness to
undermine my commitment. There are days when I just
don't feel like being with kids. When kids call, I'm
tempted to brush them off unkindly. Sometimes Saturday mornings roll around and I think, *I've worked hard for
the Lord all week. I don't want to have my quiet time today.*
That's one of Satan's primary ploys: disrupting my personal time with God. I've discovered—sometimes the
hard way—that my quiet time is the power cord between
the Lord, the source of my ministry, and me, the simple
tool He has elected to use. When I'm not plugged into
the Lord through daily prayer and Bible study, I can't get
over Satan's roadblocks of pride, insecurity, doubt, discouragement, and laziness.

It's through my daily quiet time that God reminds me
that Randy Storms and Company is not my deal, it's His
deal. He is responsible for setting the direction and getting me through the roadblocks. My job is to rely on
Him, follow His lead, and trust Him for the results. The
Lord also assures me that, despite my limitations and the
occasional disappointments and setbacks of youth work,
my ministry is making an impact on kids' lives. As long
as I make myself available to Him and to kids, He will use
me. It blows my mind that He can do so much with so
little, but I'm encouraged to stay plugged into Him to see
what He will do next.

If I had to summarize all the lessons I've learned since
my accident about myself, about my struggles, and about
God, I would use this phrase: There is life beyond the
pain. It's basically the same lesson which was drilled
into me as an athlete. In the middle of an exhausting
workout in the weight room, just when we thought our

muscles were about to self-destruct, the coach would scream this challenge: "No pain, no gain!" And when we dragged ourselves through the backbreaking two-a-day football drills during "hell week" each fall, we heard it again: "No pain, no gain!" Every athlete knows that the only way he can enjoy the glory of victory is through enduring the pain of conditioning, practice, and preparation. If you don't pay the price, you can't enjoy the fruits of victory. Similarly, I have learned that the only way I can experience true joy and fulfillment in life is by successfully going through the pain, struggles, and trials which I encounter.

I discovered a significant difference, however, between the "no pain, no gain" lesson I learned as an athlete and the "life beyond pain" lesson I learned as a quadriplegic. As a football and basketball player, I knew what kind of pain I was getting myself into *before* I signed up for the team. But when I began the obstacle course on Lookout Mountain, I had no idea of the pain and the struggles which awaited me on the other side of the mudhole. If I had, I wouldn't have run the course. And yet, even though I didn't submit myself willingly to the trials which interrupted my life on July 3, 1981, I have experienced the peace, joy, and purpose which God has provided through them.

I found two solid stepping-stones which have helped me move beyond my pain to a life of peace as a quadriplegic. The first thing I had to do was accept what had happened to me. God did not cause my injury, but He saw it coming and allowed me to dive into the mudhole anyway. I may question my poor judgment approaching the mudhole, but I can't change what happened to me, so I must accept it. I can say, "Lord, I'm not a bad guy. I was minding my own business. I didn't deserve this." But when all He says in reply is "You're right, but it happened," I must accept it. He's the potter, I'm the clay. I belong to Him and He can do anything He wants to

.e. If He allows me to break my neck, then chooses to explain why, that's His sovereign privilege.

In the weeks following my return home from Craig Hospital, I was still wrestling with "Why me?" questions. Searching for some answers, I had several conversations with Dr. John Gerstner, theologian-in-residence at our church in Wichita. Dr. Gerstner led me into the Scriptures and instructed me concerning the sovereignty of God. "God was in control on the day of your accident and He is in control today," he admonished. Once I accepted the fact that God is capable of taking care of me even when I can't take care of myself, I took a giant step toward life beyond my pain.

As I began to understand God's sovereignty, I realized that accepting my pain means being content with my lot. For months after my accident I was upset that all my career options had evaporated. *I could have been a great basketball coach or camp director, or excelled in some other career*, I pined inside. *What worthwhile job can I get as a quadriplegic?* But Dr. Gerstner helped me understand that God had me right where He wanted me. He uses garbage collectors as well as corporate executives. He can accomplish His work through peons as well as presidents. And He can use quadriplegics as well as basketball coaches. As I began to thank God for where I was and experience contentment there, I was able to start moving beyond my feelings of worthlessness.

The second stepping-stone I found which helps me experience life beyond the pain is almost a paradox of the first. Because, while I accept my struggle and express contentment with where I am, I need to move beyond my painful situation. After my accident I came to terms with the fact that the sovereign God allowed it and I couldn't change it. I learned to accept what happened to me and be content that I was still under God's control. But I didn't camp there. I began to ask God, "Where do I go from here? What's next on the program?"

For example, I accepted the fact that I was partially paralyzed, but I moved beyond the situation by developing and utilizing the physical skills I still have through strenuous exercise. Though it didn't accomplish the goal of getting me back on my feet, the two-year Myo-Flex experiment was my best shot at moving beyond my inability to walk. I continue to look for ways to push back the limits of my disability. One of my next projects is learning how to ski on a slope in Colorado which accommodates handicapped skiers.

When I think about life beyond the struggles and pain, I think about the story of an eight-year-old boy who was a rather reluctant piano student. One day the boy's mother saw in the newspaper that the great Polish pianist and composer, Ignace Paderewski, was scheduled to present a concert in their town. *I will take my son to hear Paderewski play*, she thought expectantly, *and he will be excited about practicing and playing the piano*. So she purchased the tickets and the two of them found their way to the concert hall.

Before the concert the pair was winding through the noisy crowd to their seats when the woman turned around to find that her little boy had disappeared. As the troubled mother began looking for her son, she glanced down to the stage where the massive concert grand piano awaited Paderewski's appearance. She was horrified to see her son climb up on the stage and walk toward the piano. Unruffled by the milling crowd, the boy sat down at the keyboard and began to play "Chopsticks" on the huge piano. When the crowd saw that the performer was a little boy instead of the master Paderewski, they began to boo and hiss, crying for someone to remove him from the stage.

Meanwhile offstage, Paderewski heard the simple notes of "Chopsticks" being drowned by the uproar of the incensed audience. The master walked onto the stage and a hush fell over the crowd as the little boy

...n, oblivious to his surroundings. Paderewski sat ... beside the boy on the bench and stretched his ...apping arms on either side until his large hands reached the keyboard. As the boy continued to plink the simple, two-fingered tune, Paderewski began to play a harmonious countermelody which transformed the childish "Chopsticks" into a masterpiece. And as he played, Paderewski whispered in the boy's ear, "Don't quit; keep playing. Don't quit; keep playing."

That's the message Jesus Christ keeps whispering to me in the midst of my hurts, struggles, and disappointments: "Don't quit, Randy; keep playing. Don't quit, Randy; let Me make a masterpiece out of your life." I'm humbled to know that He loves me, that He understands my pain, and that He desires to make something beautiful out of my life.

I still experience doubts about my abilities and fears about my future. There are times of disappointment when I ask, "God, is it worth it? Can You really use me to make a difference in the lives of kids today?" Often during those moments of quiet searching I roll my wheelchair out on the back porch of my Wichita home. It's my personal hideaway place. When I look up to Him as a confused, needy child, I say, "God, please love me." I sense His big, fatherly arms wrapped around me. He ties my heartstrings back together and I hear the still, small voice inside my heart saying, "I love you, Randy. Don't quit; keep playing."

Other Good Harvest House Reading

STORMIE
by *Stormie Omartian*

The childhood of singer/songwriter Stormie Omartian, marred by physical and emotional abuse, led into teen and adult years filled with tragedy. Searching for an end to the inner turmoil which constantly confronted her, Stormie found herself on the verge of suicide. In this poignant story there is help and hope for anyone who doubts the value of his or her own life. It gloriously reveals a God who can bring life out of death if we are willing to surrender to His ways.

REACHING YOUR FULL POTENTIAL
Establishing Goals in Your Life
by *Richard Furman, M.D.*

Reaching your full potential in any area of life can become a reality as you understand the importance of setting goals. Dr. Furman shares his story and the proven principles for turning dreams into reality.

GOD'S BEST FOR MY LIFE
by *Lloyd John Ogilvie*

Not since Oswald Chambers' *My Utmost for His Highest* has there been such an inspirational yet easy-to-read devotional. Dr. Ogilvie provides guidelines for maximizing your prayer and meditation time.

BEAUTIFUL SIDE OF EVIL
by Johanna Michaelsen

Hal Lindsey's sister-in-law shares her extraordinary story about her involvement in the occult and how she learned to distinguish between the beautiful side of evil and the true way of the Lord.

IT TAKES SO LITTLE TO BE ABOVE AVERAGE
by *Florence Littauer*

"Nobody wants to be average, ordinary, dull, usual, run-of-the-mill! Then why do so many of us trudge down the middle lane of life and watch the years fly by?" Insights into human behavior which will greatly inspire you and enable you to rise above the norm.

Dear Reader:

We would appreciate hearing from you regarding this Harvest House nonfiction book. It will enable us to continue to give you the best in Christian publishing.

1. What most influenced you to purchase *Between the Lightning and the Thunder*?
   ☐ Author
   ☐ Subject matter
   ☐ Backcover copy
   ☐ Recommendations
   ☐ Cover/Title
   ☐ _____

2. Where did you purchase this book?
   ☐ Christian bookstore
   ☐ General bookstore
   ☐ Department store
   ☐ Grocery store
   ☐ Other

3. Your overall rating of this book:
   ☐ Excellent ☐ Very good ☐ Good ☐ Fair ☐ Poor

4. How likely would you be to purchase other books by this author?
   ☐ Very likely
   ☐ Somewhat likely
   ☐ Not very likely
   ☐ Not at all

5. What types of books most interest you? (check all that apply)
   ☐ Women's Books
   ☐ Marriage Books
   ☐ Current Issues
   ☐ Self Help/Psychology
   ☐ Bible Studies
   ☐ Fiction
   ☐ Biographies
   ☐ Children's Books
   ☐ Youth Books
   ☐ Other _____

6. Please check the box next to your age group.
   ☐ Under 18
   ☐ 18-24
   ☐ 25-34
   ☐ 35-44
   ☐ 45-54
   ☐ 55 and over

Mail to: Editorial Director
Harvest House Publishers, Inc.
1075 Arrowsmith
Eugene, OR 97402

Name _____

Address _____

City _____ State _____ Zip _____

**Thank you for helping us to help you
in future publications!**